Cake Mix

MAGIC
In Minutes

Publications International, Ltd.

Favorite Brand Name Recipes at www.fbnr.com

Pictured on the front cover: Refreshing Lemon Cake *(page 14).*

Pictured on the back cover *(top to bottom):* Coconut Clouds *(page 74),* Banana Split Cupcakes *(page 120)* and Chocolate Cherry Cookies *(page 54).*

Microwave Cooking: Microwave ovens vary in wattage. Use the cooking times as guidelines and check for doneness before adding more time.

Preparation/Cooking Times: Preparation times are based on the approximate amount of time required to assemble the recipe before cooking, baking, chilling or serving. These times include preparation steps such as measuring, chopping and mixing. The fact that some preparations and cooking can be done simultaneously is taken into account. Preparation of optional ingredients and serving suggestions is not included.

Contents

p. 19

p. 57

p. 149

Charming Classics

Coconut Jam Cake

1 package (2-layer size)
   yellow cake mix
1 package (7 ounces)
   BAKER'S® ANGEL
   FLAKE® Coconut,
   divided
½ cup strawberry jam
1 tub (8 ounces) COOL
   WHIP® Whipped
   Topping, thawed
½ cup apricot jam
   Sliced fresh strawberries
   Canned apricot halves,
   drained
   Fresh mint leaves

HEAT oven to 350°F.

PREPARE and bake cake mix as directed on package for 2 (9-inch) round cake layers, gently stirring 1 cup coconut into batter just before pouring into pans. Cool 10 minutes; remove from pans. Cool completely on wire racks.

PLACE 1 cake layer on serving plate; spread top with strawberry jam. Spread ¾ cup whipped topping over jam; top with second cake layer. Spread top of cake with apricot jam. Frost top and side of cake with remaining whipped topping. Pat remaining coconut onto side of cake.

REFRIGERATE until ready to serve. Garnish with fruit and mint just before serving.   *Makes 12 servings*

Coconut Jam Cake

Hot Fudge Sundae Cake

1 package DUNCAN HINES®
   Moist Deluxe® Dark
   Chocolate Fudge
   Cake Mix

½ gallon brick vanilla ice
   cream

FUDGE SAUCE

   1 can (12 ounces)
      evaporated milk

1¼ cups sugar

   4 squares (1 ounce each)
      unsweetened chocolate

¼ cup butter or margarine

1½ teaspoons vanilla extract

¼ teaspoon salt

   Whipped cream and
      maraschino cherries,
      for garnish

1. Preheat oven to 350°F. Grease and flour 13×9×2-inch pan. Prepare, bake and cool cake following package directions.

2. Remove cake from pan. Split cake in half horizontally. Place bottom layer back in pan. Cut ice cream into even slices and place evenly over bottom cake layer (use all the ice cream). Place remaining cake layer over ice cream. Cover and freeze.

3. For fudge sauce, combine evaporated milk and sugar in medium saucepan. Stir constantly on medium heat until mixture comes to a rolling boil. Boil and stir for 1 minute. Add unsweetened chocolate and stir until melted. Beat over medium heat until smooth. Remove from heat. Stir in butter, vanilla and salt.

4. Cut cake into serving squares. For each serving, place cake square on plate; spoon hot fudge sauce on top. Garnish with whipped cream and maraschino cherry.

Makes 12 to 16 servings

Tip: Fudge sauce may be prepared ahead and refrigerated in tightly sealed jar. Reheat when ready to serve.

Hot Fudge Sundae Cake

Black Forest Cake

1 package (2-layer size) chocolate cake mix plus ingredients to prepare mix
2 cans (20 ounces each) tart pitted cherries, undrained
1 cup granulated sugar
¼ cup cornstarch
1½ teaspoons vanilla
Frosting (recipe follows)

1. Preheat oven to 350°F. Grease and flour two (9-inch) round cake pans; set aside.

2. Prepare cake mix according to package directions. Divide batter between prepared pans.

3. Bake 30 to 35 minutes or until wooden toothpick inserted into centers comes out clean. Cool in pans on wire racks 10 minutes. Remove from pans; cool completely on racks.

4. Meanwhile, drain cherries, reserving ½ cup juice. Combine reserved juice, cherries, sugar and cornstarch in 2-quart saucepan. Cook over low heat until thickened, stirring constantly. Stir in vanilla. Prepare Frosting.

5. With long serrated knife, split each cooled cake layer horizontally in half. Crumble one split layer; set aside.

6. Reserve 1½ cups Frosting for decorating cake; set aside. Place one cake layer on cake plate. Spread with 1 cup Frosting; top with ¾ cup cherry topping. Top with second cake layer; repeat layers of Frosting and cherry topping. Top with third cake layer.

7. Frost side of cake with remaining Frosting. Pat reserved crumbs onto frosting on side of cake. Spoon reserved frosting into pastry bag fitted with star decorator tip. Pipe around top and bottom edges of cake. Spoon remaining Cherry Topping onto top of cake. *Makes one 3-layer cake*

Frosting: Beat 3 cups cold whipping cream and ⅓ cup powdered sugar in chilled deep medium bowl with electric mixer at high speed until stiff peaks form.

Black Forest Cake

Double Chocolate Bundt Cake

1 package (about 18 ounces) chocolate cake mix

1 package (4-serving size) instant chocolate pudding mix

4 eggs, beaten

¾ cup water

¾ cup sour cream

½ cup oil

6 ounces (1 cup) semisweet chocolate chips

Powdered sugar

1. Preheat oven to 350°F. Spray 10-inch Bundt or tube pan with nonstick cooking spray.

2. Beat cake mix, pudding mix, eggs, water, sour cream and oil in large bowl with electric mixer at medium speed until ingredients are blended. Stir in chocolate chips; pour into prepared pan.

3. Bake 55 to 60 minutes or until cake springs back when lightly touched. Cool 1 hour in pan on wire rack. Invert cake onto serving plate; cool completely. Sprinkle with powdered sugar before serving.

Makes 10 to 12 servings

Festive Chocolate Chip Cookies

1 package DUNCAN HINES® Moist Deluxe® Classic White Cake Mix

¼ cup firmly packed light brown sugar

1 egg

¾ cup vegetable oil

1 package (6 ounces) semi-sweet chocolate chips

½ cup chopped pecans or walnuts

Assorted decors

1. Preheat oven to 350°F.

2. Combine cake mix, brown sugar, egg and oil in large bowl. Beat at low speed with electric mixer until blended. Stir in chocolate chips and pecans. Form dough into 1½-inch ball. Dip top of ball in decors. Place ball decor-side up on ungreased baking sheets. Repeat with remaining dough, placing balls 2 inches apart on baking sheets. Bake at 350°F 10 to 12 minutes or until light golden brown around edges. Cool 2 minutes on baking sheets. Remove to cooling racks. Cool completely. Store in airtight container.

Makes 3 to 3½ dozen cookies

Tip: Cool baking sheet completely before baking each batch of cookies.

Marbled Angel Cake

1 package (16 ounces)
angel food cake mix
¼ cup HERSHEY'S Cocoa
Chocolate Glaze (recipe
follows)

1. Place oven rack in lowest position. Heat oven to 375°F.

2. Prepare cake batter as directed on package. Transfer 4 cups batter to medium bowl; gradually fold in cocoa until well blended, being careful not to deflate batter. Alternately pour vanilla and chocolate batters into ungreased 10-inch tube pan. With knife or metal spatula, cut through batters for marble effect.

3. Bake 30 to 35 minutes or until top crust is firm and looks very dry. *Do not underbake.* Invert pan on heatproof funnel or bottle; cool completely, at least 1½ hours. Carefully run knife along side of pan to loosen cake; remove from pan. Place on serving plate; drizzle with Chocolate Glaze. Let stand until set. Store, covered, at room temperature.   *Makes 16 servings*

Chocolate Glaze: In small saucepan, combine ⅓ cup sugar and ¼ cup water. Cook over medium heat, stirring constantly, until mixture comes to a boil. Stir until sugar dissolves; remove from heat. Immediately add 1 cup HERSHEY'S MINI CHIPS® Semi-Sweet Chocolate; stir until chips are melted and mixture is smooth. Cool to desired consistency; use immediately. Makes about ⅔ cup glaze.

Fudgy Ripple Cake

1 package (18.25 ounces) yellow cake mix plus ingredients to prepare mix
1 package (3 ounces) cream cheese, softened
2 tablespoons unsweetened cocoa powder
Fudgy Glaze (recipe follows)
½ cup "M&M's"® Chocolate Mini Baking Bits

Preheat oven to 350°F. Lightly grease and flour 10-inch Bundt or ring pan; set aside. Prepare cake mix as package directs. In medium bowl combine 1½ cups prepared batter, cream cheese and cocoa powder until smooth. Pour half of yellow batter into prepared pan. Drop spoonfuls of chocolate batter over yellow batter in pan. Top with remaining yellow batter. Bake about 45 minutes or until toothpick inserted near center comes out clean. Cool completely on wire rack. Unmold cake onto serving plate. Prepare Fudgy Glaze; spread over top of cake, allowing some glaze to run over side. Sprinkle with "M&M's"® Chocolate Mini Baking Bits. Store in tightly covered container.

Makes 10 servings

Fudgy Glaze

1 square (1 ounce) semi-sweet chocolate
1 cup powdered sugar
⅓ cup unsweetened cocoa powder
3 tablespoons milk
½ teaspoon vanilla extract

Place chocolate in small microwave-safe bowl. Microwave at HIGH 30 seconds; stir. Repeat as necessary until chocolate is completely melted, stirring at 10-second intervals; set aside. In medium bowl combine powdered sugar and cocoa powder. Stir in milk, vanilla and melted chocolate until smooth.

Fudgy Ripple Cake

Refreshing Lemon Cake

1 package DUNCAN HINES®
Moist Deluxe® Butter
Recipe Golden Cake
Mix

1 container DUNCAN
HINES® Creamy Home-
Style Cream Cheese
Frosting

¾ cup purchased lemon
curd

Lemon drop candies,
crushed, for garnish
(optional)

1. Preheat oven to 375°F. Grease and flour two 8- or 9-inch round cake pans.

2. Prepare, bake and cool cake following package directions for basic recipe.

3. To assemble, place one cake layer on serving plate. Place ¼ cup Cream Cheese frosting in small resealable plastic bag. Snip off one corner. Pipe a bead of frosting on top of layer around outer edge. Fill remaining area with lemon curd. Top with second cake layer. Spread remaining frosting on sides and top of cake. Garnish top of cake with crushed lemon candies, if desired.

Makes 12 to 16 servings

Tip: You may substitute Duncan Hines® Vanilla or Vanilla Buttercream frosting for the Cream Cheese frosting, if desired.

Magical Tip

Lemon curd is a creamy mixture made of lemon juice, butter, sugar and egg yolks cooked together until it thickens. The mixture thickens even more as it cools; it is then used as a filling or topping for cakes, breads and other baked goods. Lemon curd is usually sold in jars and is found in gourmet shops and some supermarkets.

Refreshing Lemon Cake

Spicy Oatmeal Raisin Cookies

1 package DUNCAN HINES®
  Moist Deluxe® Spice
  Cake Mix
4 egg whites
1 cup uncooked
  quick-cooking oats
  (not instant or
  old-fashioned)
½ cup vegetable oil
½ cup raisins

Preheat oven to 350°F. Grease cookie sheets.

Combine cake mix, egg whites, oats and oil in large mixing bowl. Beat at low speed with electric mixer until blended. Stir in raisins. Drop by rounded teaspoonfuls onto prepared cookie sheets.

Bake 7 to 9 minutes or until lightly browned. Cool 1 minute on cookie sheets. Remove to cooling racks; cool completely.   *Makes about 4 dozen cookies*

Pudding Poke Cake

1 package (2-layer size)
  chocolate cake mix or
  cake mix with pudding
  in the mix
4 cups cold milk
2 packages (4-serving size)
  JELL-O® Vanilla Flavor
  Instant Pudding & Pie
  Filling

PREPARE and bake cake mix as directed on package for 13×9-inch baking pan. Remove from oven. Immediately poke holes down through cake to pan at 1-inch intervals with round handle of a wooden spoon. (Or poke holes with a plastic drinking straw, using turning motion to make large holes.)

POUR milk into large bowl. Add pudding mixes. Beat with wire whisk 2 minutes. Quickly pour about ½ of the thin pudding mixture evenly over warm cake and into holes. Let remaining pudding mixture stand to thicken slightly. Spoon over top of cake, swirling to frost cake.

REFRIGERATE at least 1 hour or until ready to serve.

Makes 15 servings

Prep Time: 30 minutes
Bake Time: 40 minutes
Refrigerating Time: 1 hour

Carrot Layer Cake

CAKE

- 1 package DUNCAN HINES® Moist Deluxe® Classic Yellow Cake Mix
- 4 eggs
- ½ cup vegetable oil
- 3 cups grated carrots
- 1 cup finely chopped nuts
- 2 teaspoons ground cinnamon

CREAM CHEESE FROSTING

- 1 (8-ounce) package cream cheese, softened
- ¼ cup butter or margarine, softened
- 2 teaspoons vanilla extract
- 4 cups confectioners' sugar

1. Preheat oven to 350°F. Grease and flour 2 (8- or 9-inch) round baking pans.

2. For cake, combine cake mix, eggs, oil, carrots, nuts and cinnamon in large bowl. Beat at low speed with electric mixer until moistened. Beat at medium speed for 2 minutes. Pour into pans. Bake at 350°F for 35 to 40 minutes or until toothpick inserted in centers comes out clean. Cool.

3. For frosting, place cream cheese, butter and vanilla extract in large bowl. Beat at low speed until smooth and creamy. Add confectioners' sugar gradually, beating until smooth. Add more sugar to thicken, or milk or water to thin frosting, as needed. Fill and frost cooled cake. Garnish with whole pecans.

Makes 12 to 16 servings

German Chocolate Cake

- 1 (18¼-ounce) package chocolate cake mix
- 1 cup water
- 3 eggs plus 1 egg yolk
- ½ cup vegetable oil
- 1 (14-ounce) can EAGLE® BRAND Sweetened Condensed Milk (NOT evaporated milk), divided
- 3 tablespoons butter or margarine
- ⅓ cup chopped pecans
- ⅓ cup flaked coconut
- 1 teaspoon vanilla extract

1. Preheat oven to 350°F. Grease and flour 13×9-inch baking pan. In large bowl, combine cake mix, water, 3 eggs, oil and ⅓ cup Eagle Brand. Beat at low speed until moistened; beat at high speed 2 minutes.

2. Pour into prepared pan. Bake 40 to 45 minutes or until wooden pick inserted near center comes out clean.

3. In small saucepan over medium heat, combine remaining Eagle Brand, egg yolk and butter. Cook and stir until thickened, about 6 minutes. Add pecans, coconut and vanilla; spread over warm cake. Store covered in refrigerator. *Makes 10 to 12 servings*

Prep Time: 15 minutes
Bake Time: 40 to 45 minutes

Brownie Bottom Cheesecake

CRUST

> 1 package (10 to
> 16 ounces) brownie
> mix, any variety
> (8×8 pan size)

FILLING

> 3 packages (8 ounces
> each) PHILADELPHIA®
> Cream Cheese,
> softened

> ¾ cup sugar

> 1 teaspoon vanilla

> ½ cup BREAKSTONE'S® *or*
> KNUDSEN® Sour Cream

> 3 eggs

CRUST

PREPARE and bake brownie mix as directed on package for 8-inch square pan in bottom of well-greased 9-inch springform pan.

FILLING

MIX cream cheese, sugar and vanilla with electric mixer on medium speed until well blended. Blend in sour cream. Add eggs, mixing on low speed just until blended. Pour over brownie crust.

BAKE at 325°F for 1 hour to 1 hour and 5 minutes or until center is almost set if using a silver springform pan. (Bake at 300°F for 1 hour to 1 hour and 5 minutes or until center is almost set if using a dark nonstick springform pan.) Run knife or metal spatula around rim of pan to loosen cake; cool before removing rim of pan. Refrigerate 4 hours or overnight. *Makes 12 servings*

Prep Time: 20 minutes plus refrigerating
Bake Time: 1 hour 5 minutes

Brownie Bottom Cheesecake

Marbled Chocolate Sour Cream Cake

Charming Classics

1 cup (6 ounces) NESTLÉ®
   TOLL HOUSE® Semi-
   Sweet Chocolate
   Morsels
1 package (18.5 ounces)
   yellow cake mix
4 eggs
¾ cup sour cream
½ cup vegetable oil
¼ cup water
¼ cup granulated sugar
   Powdered sugar
   (optional)

MICROWAVE morsels in medium, microwave-safe bowl on HIGH (100% power) for 1 minute; stir. Microwave at additional 10- to 20-second intervals, stirring until smooth.

COMBINE cake mix, eggs, sour cream, oil, water and granulated sugar in large mixer bowl. Beat on low speed until moistened. Beat on high speed for 2 minutes.

STIR 2 cups batter into melted chocolate. Alternately spoon batters into greased 10-cup Bundt or round tube pan.

BAKE in preheated 375°F. oven for 35 to 45 minutes or until wooden pick inserted near center comes out clean. Cool in pan for 20 minutes; invert onto wire rack to cool completely. Sprinkle with powdered sugar before serving. *Makes 24 servings*

Double Pineapple Upside-Down Cake

½ cup (1 stick) butter or
   margarine
1 cup packed brown sugar
1 (20-ounce) can pineapple
   slices, drained
   Maraschino cherry
   halves, drained
1 package DUNCAN HINES®
   Moist Deluxe®
   Pineapple Supreme
   Cake Mix
   Whipped cream

Preheat oven to 350°F.

Place butter in 13×9-inch pan. Place pan in oven to melt butter. Sprinkle with sugar. Arrange pineapple slices and maraschino cherries on sugar mixture.

Prepare cake mix as directed on package. (Do not substitute pineapple juice for water.) Pour batter evenly over fruit. Bake 50 minutes or until toothpick inserted in center comes out clean. Let stand 5 minutes. Invert onto large serving plate or cookie sheet. Serve warm with whipped cream. *Makes 12 to 16 servings*

Tip: This cake is also delicious using DUNCAN HINES® Moist Deluxe Yellow Cake Mix.

Everyone's Favorite E-Z Lemon Cake

1 package (18¼ ounces) two-layer yellow or lemon cake mix (without pudding mix preferred)

1 package (3.4 ounces) *instant* lemon pudding and pie filling

4 eggs

1 cup water

⅓ cup vegetable oil

Grated peel and juice of 1 SUNKIST® lemon (3 tablespoons juice)

E-Z Lemon Glaze (recipe follows)

In large bowl, combine cake and pudding mixes, eggs, water, oil and lemon juice with electric mixer at low speed 30 seconds. Beat at medium speed 2 minutes longer. Stir in lemon peel. Pour batter into well-greased and lightly floured Bundt pan or 10-inch tube pan.

Bake at 350°F 50 to 60 minutes or until toothpick inserted in center comes out clean. Cool on wire rack 15 minutes. With narrow spatula or knife, loosen around tube and sides and invert onto cake plate. While still warm, pierce top all over with long two-prong fork or wooden skewer. Spread top with half of E-Z Lemon Glaze. Cool completely. Spoon remaining glaze over cake, allowing some to drizzle over sides.

Makes 16 servings

E-Z Lemon Glaze: In small bowl, combine 1 cup confectioners' sugar, juice of ½ SUNKIST® lemon (1½ tablespoons) and ½ tablespoon water.

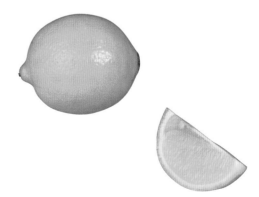

Butter Pecan Banana Cake

CAKE

1 package DUNCAN HINES®
   Moist Deluxe® Butter
   Recipe Golden Cake
   Mix

4 eggs

1 cup mashed ripe bananas
   (about 3 medium)

¾ cup vegetable oil

½ cup granulated sugar

¼ cup milk

1 teaspoon vanilla extract

1 cup chopped pecans

FROSTING

1 cup coarsely chopped
   pecans

¼ cup butter or margarine

1 container DUNCAN
   HINES® Vanilla Frosting

Preheat oven to 325°F. Grease and flour 10-inch Bundt or tube pan.

Combine cake mix, eggs, bananas, oil, sugar, milk and vanilla extract in large mixing bowl. Beat at low speed with electric mixer until moistened. Beat at medium speed for 2 minutes. Stir in 1 cup chopped pecans. Pour into prepared pan. Bake 50 to 60 minutes or until toothpick inserted in center comes out clean. Cool in pan 25 minutes. Invert onto cooling rack. Cool completely.

Place 1 cup coarsely chopped pecans and butter in skillet. Cook on medium heat, stirring until pecans are toasted. Combine nut mixture and frosting in small bowl. Cool until spreading consistency. Frost cake.

Makes 12 to 16 servings

Magical Tip

To get the most flavor in your banana cake, it's important to use bananas that are ripe. Look for evenly colored yellow bananas with flecks of tiny brown spots—unripe bananas will not have these flecks and will still be green at the tips. To ripen bananas, store them uncovered at room temperature. To speed up the ripening, place the bananas in a perforated brown paper bag with a ripe apple.

Butter Pecan Banana Cake

Abracadabra
Cakes

Easy Cappuccino Cake

1 package (2-layer size) white cake mix

4 tablespoons MAXWELL HOUSE® Instant Coffee, divided

¼ cup milk plus 1 tablespoon milk

4 squares BAKER'S® Semi-Sweet Baking Chocolate, melted

2 tubs (8 ounces each) COOL WHIP® Whipped Topping, thawed, divided

HEAT oven to 350°F.

PREPARE and bake cake mix as directed on package for 8- or 9-inch round pans, adding 2 tablespoons instant coffee to cake mix.

POUR ¼ cup milk and 1 tablespoon instant coffee into small bowl, stirring until coffee is dissolved. Slowly stir into melted chocolate until smooth. Cool completely. Gently stir in 1 tub of whipped topping. Refrigerate 20 minutes, or until well chilled.

MEANWHILE, mix 1 tablespoon milk and 1 tablespoon coffee until dissolved. Gently stir into remaining tub of whipped topping.

COVER one cake layer with chocolate mixture. Place second cake layer on top. Frost top and side of cake with coffee-flavored whipped topping. Refrigerate until ready to serve. *Makes 14 servings*

Variation: If desired, omit the coffee for a delicious plain chocolate filled layer cake.

Prep Time: 25 minutes

Easy Cappuccino Cake

Banana-Coconut Crunch Cake

CAKE

> 1 package DUNCAN HINES®
> Moist Deluxe® Banana
> Supreme Cake Mix
>
> 1 package (4-serving size)
> banana instant
> pudding and pie
> filling mix
>
> 1 can (16 ounces) fruit
> cocktail, in juices,
> undrained
>
> 4 eggs
>
> ¼ cup vegetable oil
>
> 1 cup flaked coconut
>
> ½ cup chopped pecans
>
> ½ cup firmly packed brown
> sugar

GLAZE

> ¾ cup granulated sugar
>
> ½ cup butter or margarine
>
> ½ cup evaporated milk
>
> 1⅓ cups flaked coconut

1. Preheat oven to 350°F. Grease and flour 13×9×2-inch pan.

2. For cake, combine cake mix, pudding mix, fruit cocktail with juice, eggs and oil in large bowl. Beat at medium speed with electric mixer for 4 minutes. Stir in 1 cup coconut. Pour into pan. Combine pecans and brown sugar in small bowl. Stir until well mixed. Sprinkle over batter. Bake at 350°F for 45 to 50 minutes or until toothpick inserted in center comes out clean.

3. For glaze, combine granulated sugar, butter and evaporated milk in medium saucepan. Bring to boil. Cook for 2 minutes, stirring occasionally. Remove from heat. Stir in 1⅓ cups coconut. Pour over warm cake. Serve warm or at room temperature.

Makes 12 to 16 servings

Tip: Assemble all ingredients and utensils together before beginning the recipe.

• Magical Tip

If your brown sugar has hardened, it can be softened quickly and easily in a microwave oven. Place 1 cup brown sugar in a microwavable dish, cover and heat at HIGH for 30 to 60 seconds. Check the sugar frequently to be sure it doesn't start to melt.

Banana-Coconut Crunch Cake

Citrus Poppy Seed Cake

CAKE

WESSON® No-Stick
  Cooking Spray
1⅓ cups orange juice
½ cup WESSON® Vegetable
  Oil
3 eggs
1 box (18.25 ounces)
  lemon cake mix
2 tablespoons poppy seeds
Grated peel from
  1 orange and 1 lemon

ICING

2 cups powdered sugar,
  sifted
2 to 3 tablespoons orange
  juice
Dash salt
½ tablespoons poppy seeds
  (optional)
Grated peel from
  1 orange and 1 lemon

For cake, preheat oven to 350°F. Lightly spray Bundt pan with Wesson Cooking Spray. Using electric mixer, beat orange juice, oil and eggs; mix well. Slowly add cake mix to batter; mix on low speed until just moistened. Beat on medium speed for 2 minutes. Fold in poppy seeds and orange and lemon peel. Pour batter into Bundt pan; bake for 40 to 45 minutes or until toothpick inserted into cake comes out clean. Cool on wire rack for 10 minutes. Invert cake onto cake plate; let cool completely. Spoon icing over cake and top with additional orange and lemon peel, if desired.

For icing, combine all icing ingredients; mix well. Icing should be moderately thick but not thin enough to run off cake. Add more sugar or juice to achieve desired consistency. *Makes 12 servings*

Country Oat Cake

CAKE

- 1 package (18.5 ounces) spice cake mix
- 1 cup QUAKER® Oats (quick or old fashioned, uncooked)
- 1 carton (8 ounces) plain lowfat yogurt
- 3 eggs or ¾ cup egg substitute
- ¼ cup vegetable oil
- ¼ cup water
- 1 ½ cups peeled, finely chopped apples (about 2 medium)

TOPPING

- 1 cup QUAKER® Oats (quick or old fashioned, uncooked)
- ½ cup firmly packed brown sugar
- ¼ cup (½ stick) margarine or butter, softened
- ½ teaspoon ground cinnamon
- Whipped cream (optional)

Heat oven to 350°F. Grease and flour 13×9-inch baking pan. For cake, combine cake mix, oats, yogurt, eggs, oil and water. Blend on low speed of electric mixer until moistened; mix at medium speed for 2 minutes. Stir in apples. Pour into prepared pan.

For topping, combine oats, brown sugar, margarine and cinnamon; mix well. Sprinkle evenly over batter. Bake 40 to 45 minutes or until wooden pick inserted in center comes out clean. Serve warm or at room temperature with whipped cream, if desired.

Makes 16 servings

Sock-It-To-Me Cake

STREUSEL FILLING

- 1 package DUNCAN HINES® Moist Deluxe® Butter Recipe Golden Cake Mix, divided
- 2 tablespoons brown sugar
- 2 teaspoons ground cinnamon
- 1 cup finely chopped pecans

CAKE

- 4 eggs
- 1 cup dairy sour cream
- 1/3 cup vegetable oil
- 1/4 cup water
- 1/4 cup granulated sugar

GLAZE

- 1 cup confectioners' sugar
- 1 or 2 tablespoons milk

1. Preheat oven to 375°F. Grease and flour 10-inch tube pan.

2. For streusel filling, combine 2 tablespoons cake mix, brown sugar and cinnamon in medium bowl. Stir in pecans. Set aside.

3. For cake, combine remaining cake mix, eggs, sour cream, oil, water and granulated sugar in large bowl. Beat at medium speed with electric mixer 2 minutes. Pour two-thirds of batter into pan. Sprinkle with streusel filling. Spoon remaining batter evenly over filling. Bake at 375°F 45 to 55 minutes or until toothpick inserted in center comes out clean. Cool in pan 25 minutes. Invert onto serving plate. Cool completely.

4. For glaze, combine confectioners' sugar and milk in small bowl. Stir until smooth. Drizzle over cake.

Makes 12 to 16 servings

Tip: For a quick glaze, place 1/2 cup Duncan Hines® Creamy Homestyle Vanilla Frosting in small microwave-safe bowl. Microwave at HIGH (100% power) 10 seconds; add 5 to 10 seconds, if needed. Stir until smooth and thin.

Sock-It-To-Me Cake

Elegant Chocolate Angel Torte

⅓ cup HERSHEY'S Cocoa
1 package (about 16 ounces) angel food cake mix
2 envelopes (1.3 ounces each) dry whipped topping mix
1 cup cold nonfat milk
1 teaspoon vanilla extract
1 cup strawberry purée*
Strawberries

*Mash 2 cups sliced fresh strawberries (or frozen berries, thawed) in blender or food processor. Cover; blend until smooth. Purée should measure 1 cup.

1. Move oven rack to lowest position.

2. Sift cocoa over dry cake mix in large bowl; stir to blend. Proceed with mixing cake as directed on package. Bake and cool as directed for 10-inch tube pan. Carefully run knife along side of pan to loosen cake; remove from pan. Using serrated knife, slice cake horizontally into four layers.

3. Prepare whipped topping mix as directed on package, using 1 cup nonfat milk and 1 teaspoon vanilla. Fold in strawberry purée.

4. Place bottom cake layer on serving plate; spread with ¼ of strawberry topping. Set next cake layer on top; spread with ¼ of topping. Continue layering cake and topping. Garnish with strawberries. Refrigerate until ready to serve. Slice cake with sharp serrated knife, cutting with gentle sawing motion. Cover; refrigerate leftover cake.   *Makes about 16 servings*

Prep Time: 30 minutes
Bake Time: 45 minutes
Cool Time: 2 hours

Elegant Chocolate Angel Torte

Dump Cake

1 (20-ounce) can crushed pineapple with juice, undrained

1 (21-ounce) can cherry pie filling

1 package DUNCAN HINES® Moist Deluxe® Yellow Cake Mix

1 cup chopped pecans or walnuts

½ cup (1 stick) butter or margarine, cut into thin slices

Preheat oven to 350°F. Grease 13×9-inch pan.

Dump pineapple with juice into pan. Spread evenly. Dump in pie filling. Spread evenly. Sprinkle cake mix evenly over cherry layer. Sprinkle pecans over cake mix. Dot with butter. Bake 50 minutes or until top is lightly browned. Serve warm or at room temperature.

Makes 12 to 16 servings

Tip: You can use DUNCAN HINES® Moist Deluxe® Pineapple Supreme Cake Mix in place of Moist Deluxe® Yellow Cake Mix.

Pistachio Pudding Cake

1 package (2-layer size) yellow cake mix*

1 package (4-serving size) JELL-O® Pistachio Flavor Instant Pudding & Pie Filling

4 eggs

1¼ cups water*

¼ cup oil

½ teaspoon almond extract

7 drops green food coloring (optional)

Powdered sugar

*Or use cake mix with pudding in the mix and reduce water to 1 cup.

HEAT oven to 350°F.

PLACE all ingredients except powdered sugar in large bowl. Beat with electric mixer on low speed just to moisten. Beat on medium speed 4 minutes. Pour into greased and floured 10-inch fluted tube or tube pan.

BAKE 50 to 55 minutes or until toothpick inserted in center comes out clean.

REMOVE cake from oven. Cool 15 minutes; remove from pan. Cool completely on wire rack. Dust with powdered sugar just before serving.

Makes 12 servings

Prep Time: 20 minutes
Bake Time: 55 minutes

Dump Cake

Orange Glow Bundt Cake

1 (18.25-ounce) package
  moist yellow cake mix
1 tablespoon grated
  orange peel
1 cup orange juice
¼ cup sugar
1 tablespoon TABASCO®
  brand Pepper Sauce
1¾ cups confectioners' sugar

Preheat oven to 375°F. Grease 12-cup Bundt pan. Prepare cake mix according to package directions, adding orange peel to batter. Bake 35 to 40 minutes or until toothpick inserted near center of cake comes out clean.

Meanwhile, heat orange juice, sugar and TABASCO® Sauce to boiling in 1-quart saucepan. Reduce heat to low; simmer, uncovered, 5 minutes. Remove from heat. Reserve ¼ cup orange juice mixture for glaze.

Remove cake from oven. With wooden skewer, poke holes in cake (in pan) in several places. Spoon remaining orange juice mixture over cake. Cool cake in pan 10 minutes. Carefully invert cake onto wire rack to cool completely.

Combine reserved ¼ cup orange juice mixture and confectioners' sugar in small bowl until smooth. Place cake on platter; spoon glaze over cake. Garnish with clusters of dried cranberries, mint leaves and grated orange peel.

Makes 12 servings

Magical Tip

Before grating the peel, scrub the orange thoroughly to remove pesticide residues as well as the wax coating. The peel can be grated with the fine side of a box grater. When grating orange peel, grate only the outer orange layer of the skin, which is very sweet and flavorful. Avoid grating into the white pith, as it is bitter tasting.

Orange Glow Bundt Cake

Banana Jewel Cake

1 box (18 ounces) vanilla-
  flavored cake mix
1 cup water
¼ cup orange juice
2 tablespoons grated
  orange peel
¼ cup sugar
1½ cups DOLE® Fresh
  Cranberries
3 DOLE® Bananas, sliced

• Prepare cake mix as directed, except add only 1 cup water. Pour into 13×9-inch baking pan.

• Heat orange juice and grated peel in medium saucepan until hot. Add sugar and stir to dissolve. Add cranberries and simmer until skins burst. Add bananas. Continue cooking for 1 minute. Remove from heat.

• Evenly spoon cranberry-banana mixture over cake. *Do not stir.*

• Bake at 350°F, 35 to 40 minutes or until lightly browned. Garnish with fresh cranberries and orange twist, if desired. *Makes 12 servings*

Prep Time: 15 minutes
Bake Time: 35 minutes

Easy Carrot Cake

1¼ cups MIRACLE WHIP®
  Salad Dressing
1 (2-layer size) yellow
  cake mix
4 eggs
¼ cup cold water
2 teaspoons ground
  cinnamon
2 cups finely shredded
  carrots
½ cup chopped PLANTERS®
  Walnuts
1 (16-ounce) container
  ready-to-spread cream
  cheese frosting

• Beat salad dressing, cake mix, eggs, water and cinnamon in large bowl with electric mixer at medium speed until well blended. Stir in carrots and walnuts.

• Pour batter into greased 13×9-inch baking pan.

• Bake at 350°F for 35 to 40 minutes or until wooden toothpick inserted in center comes out clean. Cool completely. Spread cake with frosting. Garnish as desired. *Makes 12 servings*

Prep Time: 15 minutes
Bake Time: 35 minutes

Luscious Lime Angel Food Cake Rolls

1 package (16 ounces) angel food cake mix
2 drops green food coloring (optional)
2 containers (8 ounces each) lime-flavored nonfat sugar-free yogurt
Lime slices (optional)

1. Preheat oven to 350°F. Line two 17×11¼×1-inch jelly-roll pans with parchment or waxed paper; set aside.

2. Prepare angel food cake mix according to package directions. Divide batter evenly between prepared pans. Draw knife through batter to remove large air bubbles. Bake 12 minutes or until cakes are lightly browned and toothpick inserted in centers comes out clean.

3. Invert each cake onto separate clean towel. Starting at short end, roll up warm cake, jelly-roll fashion, with towel inside. Cool cakes completely.

4. Place 1 to 2 drops green food coloring in each container of yogurt, if desired; stir well. Unroll cake; remove towel. Spread each cake with 1 container yogurt, leaving 1-inch border. Roll up cake; place seam side down. Slice each cake roll into 8 pieces. Garnish with lime slices, if desired. Serve immediately or refrigerate.

Makes 16 servings

Fruity Pound Cake

1 package (4-serving size)
JELL-O® Brand Lemon
Flavor Gelatin Dessert

1 teaspoon grated lemon
or orange peel

1 package (2-layer size)
white cake mix or cake
mix with pudding in
the mix

¾ cup water

¼ cup oil

4 eggs

Fluffy Pudding Frosting
(recipe follows)

ADD gelatin and grated peel to cake mix.

PREPARE and bake cake mix as directed on package in two 8- or 9-inch round cake pans. Cool 15 minutes; remove from pans. Cool completely on wire racks. Fill and frost with Fluffy Pudding Frosting. Decorate as desired. *Makes 12 servings*

Fluffy Pudding Frosting: Pour 1 cup cold milk into medium bowl. Add 1 package (4-serving size) JELL-O® Instant Pudding & Pie Filling, any flavor, and ¼ cup powdered sugar. Beat with wire whisk 2 minutes. Gently stir in 1 tub (8 ounces) COOL WHIP® Whipped Topping, thawed. Spread onto cake at once. Makes about 4 cups or enough for two 8- or 9-inch layers.

Prep Time: 30 minutes
Bake Time: 40 minutes

Magical Tip

Store lemons in a plastic bag in the refrigerator for up to three weeks. Check them periodically for signs of mold. A cut lemon tightly wrapped in plastic will keep for two or three days before its flavor begins to deteriorate. One lemon yields 3 tablespoons juice and about 2 teaspoons grated peel.

Fruity Pound Cake

Take-Along Cake

1 package DUNCAN HINES®
Moist Deluxe® Swiss
Chocolate Cake Mix

1 (12-ounce) package
semisweet chocolate
chips

1 cup miniature
marshmallows

¼ cup butter or margarine,
melted

½ cup packed brown sugar

½ cup chopped pecans or
walnuts

Preheat oven to 350°F. Grease and flour 13×9-inch baking pan.

Prepare cake mix as directed on package. Add chips and marshmallows to batter. Pour into prepared pan. Drizzle melted butter over batter. Sprinkle with sugar and top with pecans. Bake 45 to 55 minutes or until toothpick inserted in center comes out clean. Serve warm or cool completely in pan. *Makes 12 to 16 servings*

Tip: To keep leftover pecans fresh, store them in the freezer in an airtight container.

Cherry-Mallow Cake

4 cups miniature
marshmallows (about
¾ of 10½-ounce
package)

1 (18.25-ounce) package
yellow cake mix

1 (21-ounce) can cherry
pie filling

Spray 13×9×2-inch baking pan with vegetable cooking spray. Place marshmallows evenly in bottom of pan.

Prepare cake mix according to package directions. Pour batter over marshmallows. Spoon cherry filling evenly over cake batter.

Bake in preheated 350°F oven 30 to 40 minutes. Top of cake will be bubbly and marshmallows will be sticky. Let cool before serving. *Makes 15 servings*

Favorite recipe from **Cherry Marketing Institute**

Take-Along Cake

Chocolate Angel Food Dessert

1 package DUNCAN HINES®
Angel Food Cake Mix

16 large marshmallows

½ cup milk

1 package (11 ounces) milk
chocolate chips

1 pint whipping cream

¼ cup semisweet chocolate
chips

1½ teaspoons shortening

1. Preheat oven to 375°F. Prepare, bake and cool cake following package directions.

2. Melt marshmallows and milk in heavy saucepan over low heat. Remove from heat; stir in milk chocolate chips until melted. Cool to room temperature. Beat whipping cream in large bowl until stiff peaks form. Fold cooled chocolate mixture into whipped cream. Refrigerate until spreading consistency.

3. To assemble, split cake horizontally into 3 even layers. Place 1 cake layer on serving plate. Spread with one-fourth of frosting. Repeat with second layer. Top with third layer. Frost side and top with remaining frosting. Refrigerate.

4. For drizzle, place semisweet chocolate chips and shortening in 1-cup glass measuring cup. Microwave at MEDIUM (50% power) for 1 minute. Stir until smooth. Drizzle melted chocolate around outer top edge of cake, allowing mixture to run down side unevenly. Refrigerate until ready to serve.

Makes 12 to 16 servings

Chocolate Angel Food Dessert

Butterscotch Banana Cake

1⅔ cups (11-ounce package)
NESTLÉ® TOLL HOUSE®
Butterscotch Flavored
Morsels, divided

1 package (18.5 ounces)
yellow cake mix

4 large eggs

¾ cup (2 medium) mashed
ripe bananas

½ cups vegetable oil

¼ cup water

¼ cup granulated sugar

PREHEAT oven to 375°F. Grease 10-cup bundt or round tube pan.

MICROWAVE *1⅓ cups* morsels in medium, microwave-safe bowl on MEDIUM-HIGH (70%) power for 1 minute; stir. Microwave for additional 10- to 20-second intervals, stirring until smooth. Combine cake mix, eggs, bananas, vegetable oil, water and granulated sugar in large mixer bowl. Beat on low speed until moistened. Beat on high speed for 2 minutes. Stir *2 cups* batter into melted morsels. Alternately spoon batters into prepared pan.

BAKE for 35 to 45 minutes or until wooden pick inserted in cake comes out clean. Cool in pan for 20 minutes; invert onto wire rack to cool completely.

PLACE *remaining* morsels in small, *heavy-duty* plastic bag. Microwave on MEDIUM-HIGH (70%) power for 30 seconds; knead. Microwave for additional 10- to 20-second intervals. kneading until smooth. Cut tiny corner from bag; squeeze to drizzle over cake.

Makes 24 servings

Lemon Sour Cream Pound Cake with Lemon Glaze

CAKE

 1 package (2-layer size)
  yellow cake mix or
  cake mix with pudding
  in the mix

 1 package (2.9 ounces)
  JELL-O® Lemon Flavor
  Cook & Serve Pudding
  & Pie Filling (not
  Instant)

 1 container (8 ounces)
  BREAKSTONE'S® Sour
  Cream

 ⅓ cup oil

 4 eggs

GLAZE

 1 cup powdered sugar

 ¼ cup lemon juice

 2 tablespoons butter or
  margarine, melted

 1 teaspoon water

HEAT oven to 350°F.

PLACE cake mix, pudding mix, sour cream, oil and eggs in large bowl. Beat with electric mixer on medium speed 4 minutes. Pour into greased and floured 10-inch tube or fluted tube pan.

BAKE 55 to 60 minutes or until toothpick inserted in center comes out clean. Meanwhile, mix powdered sugar, lemon juice, butter and water until smooth.

REMOVE cake from oven. Cool 15 minutes; remove from pan. Place on wire rack. Poke cake all over with skewer. Spoon glaze over warm cake. Dust cooled cake with additional powdered sugar, if desired.

Makes 12 servings

Prep Time: 30 minutes
Bake Time: 1 hour

Pumpkin Crunch Cake

 1 package (18.25 ounces)
  yellow cake mix,
  divided

 2 eggs

 1⅔ cups LIBBY'S® Pumpkin
  Pie Mix

 2 teaspoons pumpkin pie
  spice

 ⅓ cup flaked coconut

 ¼ cup chopped nuts

 3 tablespoons butter or
  margarine, softened

COMBINE *3 cups* cake mix, eggs, pumpkin pie mix and pumpkin pie spice in large mixer bowl. Beat on low speed until moistened. Beat on medium speed for 2 minutes. Pour into greased 13×9-inch baking pan.

COMBINE *remaining* cake mix, coconut and nuts in small bowl; cut in butter with pastry blender or two knives until mixture is crumbly. Sprinkle over batter.

BAKE in preheated 350°F. oven for 30 to 35 minutes or until wooden pick inserted in center comes out clean. Cool in pan on wire rack. *Makes 20 servings*

Strawberry Pound Cake

1 package DUNCAN HINES®
   Moist Deluxe®
   Strawberry Supreme
   Cake Mix
1 (4-serving size) package
   vanilla-flavor instant
   pudding and pie filling
   mix
4 eggs
1 cup water
⅓ cup vegetable oil
1 cup miniature semisweet
   chocolate chips
⅔ cup DUNCAN HINES®
   Creamy Home-Style
   Chocolate Butter
   Cream Frosting

Preheat oven to 350°F. Grease and flour 10-inch Bundt pan.

Combine cake mix, pudding mix, eggs, water and oil in large mixing bowl. Beat at low speed with electric mixer until moistened. Beat at medium speed for 2 minutes. Stir in chips. Pour into prepared pan. Bake 55 to 60 minutes or until toothpick inserted in center comes out clean. Cool in pan 25 minutes. Invert onto cooling rack. Cool completely.

Place frosting in 1-cup glass measuring cup. Microwave at HIGH for 10 to 15 seconds. Stir until smooth. Drizzle over top of cooled cake.

Makes 12 to 16 servings

Tip: Store leftover chocolate buttercream frosting, covered, in refrigerator. Spread frosting between graham crackers for a quick snack.

· Magical Tip

To test deep cakes such as Bundt cakes for doneness, use a long wooden skewer (generally available in supermarkets). If these are not available, a piece of uncooked spaghetti can also be used. Because home oven temperatures can vary, always test a cake for doneness 5 to 10 minutes before the end of the suggested baking time.

Strawberry Pound Cake

Fruity JELL-O® Cake

2 cups chopped
  strawberries
1 can (20 ounces) crushed
  pineapple, drained
1 package (8-serving size)
  or 2 packages
  (4-serving size each)
  JELL-O® Brand
  Strawberry Flavor
  Gelatin
3 cups miniature
  marshmallows
1 package (2-layer size)
  white cake mix
2 eggs

HEAT oven to 350°F.

ARRANGE fruit on bottom of 13×9-inch pan.
Sprinkle with gelatin. Cover with marshmallows.

PREPARE cake mix as directed on package, omitting
oil and using 2 eggs and water as specified. Spread
batter over mixture in pan.

BAKE 50 to 55 minutes. Remove to rack; cool
15 minutes. Serve warm with thawed COOL WHIP®
Whipped Topping, if desired.   *Makes 24 servings*

Prep Time: 15 minutes
Bake Time: 55 minutes

Sinfully Simple Chocolate Cake

1 package (18.25 ounces)
  chocolate cake mix
  plus ingredients to
  prepare mix
1 cup whipping cream,
  chilled
⅓ cup chocolate syrup
  Fresh fruit for garnish
  (optional)

Prepare cake mix according to package directions for
two 8- or 9-inch layers. Cool layers completely.

Beat whipping cream with electric mixer at high speed
until it begins to thicken. Gradually add choclate syrup;
continue beating until soft peaks form.

To assemble, place one cake layer on serving plate;
spread half of whipped cream mixture over top. Set
second cake layer on top; spread remaining whipped
cream mixture over top. Garnish, if desired. Store in
refrigerator.   *Makes 12 servings*

Fruity JELL-O® Cake

Fudge Ribbon Cake

1 (18¼-ounce) package
    chocolate cake mix
1 (8-ounce) package cream
    cheese, softened
2 tablespoons butter or
    margarine, softened
1 tablespoon cornstarch
1 (14-ounce) can EAGLE®
    BRAND Sweetened
    Condensed Milk (NOT
    evaporated milk)
1 egg
1 teaspoon vanilla extract
    Chocolate Glaze (recipe
    follows)

1. Preheat oven to 350°F. Grease and flour 13×9-inch baking pan. Prepare cake mix as package directs. Pour batter into prepared pan.

2. In small bowl, beat cream cheese, butter and cornstarch until fluffy. Gradually beat in Eagle Brand. Add egg and vanilla; beat until smooth. Spoon evenly over cake batter.

3. Bake 40 minutes or until wooden pick inserted near center comes out clean. Cool. Prepare Chocolate Glaze and drizzle over cake. Store covered in refrigerator.

Makes 10 to 12 servings

Chocolate Glaze: In small saucepan over low heat, melt 1 (1-ounce) square unsweetened or semi-sweet chocolate and 1 tablespoon butter or margarine with 2 tablespoons water. Remove from heat. Stir in ¾ cup powdered sugar and ½ teaspoon vanilla extract. Stir until smooth and well blended. Makes about ⅓ cup.

Fudge Ribbon Bundt Cake: Preheat oven to 350°F. Grease and flour 10-inch Bundt pan. Prepare cake mix as package directs. Pour batter into prepared pan. Prepare cream cheese topping as directed above; spoon evenly over batter. Bake 50 to 55 minutes or until wooden pick inserted near center comes out clean. Cool 10 minutes. Remove from pan. Cool. Prepare Chocolate Glaze and drizzle over cake. Store covered in refrigerator.

Prep Time: 20 minutes
Bake Time: 40 minutes

Fudge Ribbon Cake

Cookies

Chocolate Cherry Cookies

1 package (8 ounces)
  sugar-free low-fat
  chocolate cake mix

3 tablespoons fat-free
  (skim) milk

½ teaspoon almond extract

10 maraschino cherries,
  rinsed, drained and cut
  into halves

2 tablespoons white
  chocolate chips

½ teaspoon vegetable oil

Preheat oven to 350°F. Spray baking sheets with nonstick cooking spray; set aside.

Beat cake mix, milk and almond extract in medium bowl with electric mixer at low speed. Increase speed to medium when mixture looks crumbly; beat 2 minutes or until smooth dough forms. (Dough will be very sticky.)

Coat hands with cooking spray. Shape dough into 1-inch balls. Place balls 2½ inches apart on prepared baking sheets. Flatten each ball slightly. Place cherry half in center of each cookie.

Bake 8 to 9 minutes or until cookies lose their shininess and tops begin to crack. Do not overbake. Remove to wire racks; cool completely.

Heat white chocolate chips and oil in small saucepan over very low heat until chips melt. Drizzle cookies with melted chips. Allow drizzle to set before serving.

Makes 20 cookies

Chocolate Cherry Cookies

Lemon Crumb Bars

1 (18¼-ounce) package lemon or yellow cake mix

½ cup (1 stick) butter or margarine, softened

1 egg plus 3 egg yolks

2 cups finely crushed saltine crackers (¼ pound)

1 (14-ounce) can EAGLE® BRAND® Sweetened Condensed Milk (NOT evaporated milk)

½ cup REALEMON® Lemon Juice From Concentrate

1. Preheat oven to 350°F. Grease 15×10×1-inch baking pan. In large bowl, combine cake mix, butter and 1 egg; mix well (mixture will be crumbly). Stir in cracker crumbs. Reserve 2 cups crumb mixture. Press remaining crumb mixture firmly on bottom of prepared pan. Bake 15 minutes.

2. Meanwhile, in medium bowl, combine egg yolks, Eagle Brand and RealLemon; mix well. Spread evenly over baked crust.

3. Top with reserved crumb mixture. Bake 20 minutes or until firm. Cool. Cut into bars. Store covered in refrigerator. *Makes 36 to 48 bars*

Prep Time: 30 minutes
Bake Time: 35 minutes

Quick Chocolate Softies

1 package (18.25 ounces) devil's food cake mix

⅓ cup water

¼ cup butter, softened

1 egg

1 cup white chocolate chips

½ cup coarsely chopped walnuts

Preheat oven to 350°F. Grease cookie sheets. Combine cake mix, water, butter and egg in large bowl. Beat with electric mixer at low speed until moistened. Increase speed to medium; beat 1 minute. (Dough will be thick.) Stir in white chocolate chips and nuts; mix until well blended. Drop dough by heaping teaspoonfuls 2 inches apart onto prepared cookie sheets.

Bake 10 to 12 minutes or until set. Let cookies stand on cookie sheets 1 minute. Remove cookies to wire racks; cool completely. *Makes about 4 dozen cookies*

Lemon Crumb Bars

Orange Pecan Gems

1 package DUNCAN HINES®
  Moist Deluxe® Orange
  Supreme Cake Mix

1 container (8 ounces)
  vanilla low fat yogurt

1 egg

2 tablespoons butter or
  margarine, softened

1 cup finely chopped
  pecans

1 cup pecan halves

1. Preheat oven to 350°F. Grease cookie sheets.

2. Combine cake mix, yogurt, egg, butter and chopped pecans in large bowl. Beat at low speed with electric mixer until blended. Drop by rounded teaspoonfuls 2 inches apart onto prepared cookie sheets. Press pecan half onto center of each cookie. Bake at 350°F for 11 to 13 minutes or until golden brown. Cool 1 minute on cookie sheets. Remove to cooling racks. Cool completely. Store in airtight container.

Makes 4½ to 5 dozen cookies

Magical Tip

Nuts can be chopped very quickly in the food processor using the metal blade. Simply place 1 cup whole nuts or large nut pieces in the bowl and process using quick on/off pulses until the nuts reach the desired texture. Be careful not to overprocess, or you'll end up with nut paste.

Chocolate Caramel Brownies

1 package (18.25 ounces) chocolate cake mix

1 cup chopped nuts

½ cup (1 stick) butter or margarine, melted

1 cup NESTLÉ® CARNATION® Evaporated Milk, divided

35 (10-ounce package) caramels, unwrapped

1 package (12 ounces) NESTLÉ® TOLL HOUSE® Semi-Sweet Chocolate Morsels

PREHEAT oven to 350°F.

COMBINE cake mix and nuts in large bowl. Stir in butter. Stir in ⅔ *cup* evaporated milk (batter will be thick). Spread *half* of batter into greased 13×9-inch baking pan.

BAKE for 15 minutes.

HEAT caramels and *remaining* evaporated milk in small saucepan over low heat, stirring constantly, until caramels are melted. Sprinkle morsels over brownie; drizzle with caramel mixture.

DROP *remaining* batter by heaping teaspoon over caramel mixture.

BAKE for 25 to 30 minutes or until center is set. Cool in pan on wire rack.   *Makes 24 brownies*

Variation: For Rich Chocolate Butterscotch Brownies, pour 12.25-ounce jar of butterscotch-flavored topping over Nestlé® Toll House® Semi-Sweet Chocolate Morsels, instead of melting caramels with ⅓ cup evaporated milk.

Pinwheel Cookies

½ cup shortening plus
   additional for greasing
⅓ cup plus 1 tablespoon
   butter, softened and
   divided
2 egg yolks
½ teaspoon vanilla
1 package DUNCAN HINES®
   Moist Deluxe® Fudge
   Marble Cake Mix

1. Combine ½ cup shortening, ⅓ cup butter, egg yolks and vanilla in large bowl. Mix at low speed of electric mixer until blended. Set aside cocoa packet from cake mix. Gradually add cake mix. Blend well.

2. Divide dough in half. Add cocoa packet and remaining 1 tablespoon butter to one half of dough. Knead until well blended and chocolate colored.

3. Roll out yellow dough between two pieces of waxed paper into 18×12×⅛-inch rectangle. Repeat for chocolate dough. Remove top pieces of waxed paper from chocolate and yellow doughs. Place yellow dough directly on top of chocolate dough. Remove remaining layers of waxed paper. Roll up jelly-roll fashion, beginning at wide side. Refrigerate 2 hours.

4. Preheat oven to 350°F. Grease cookie sheets.

5. Cut dough into ⅛-inch slices. Place sliced dough 1 inch apart on prepared cookie sheets. Bake 9 to 11 minutes or until lightly browned. Cool 5 minutes on cookie sheets. Remove to cooling racks.

Makes about 3½ dozen cookies

Magical Tip

Before chilling, wrap the roll of dough securely in plastic wrap to keep air from penetrating the dough and causing it to dry out. Once the roll is firm, use gentle pressure and a back-and-forth sawing motion to cut the roll into slices with a sharp knife—this will help the cookies keep their nice round shape. Rotating the roll while slicing also prevents one side from flattening.

Pinwheel Cookies

Creamy Lemon Bars

1 package (2-layer size)
   lemon cake mix
3 large eggs, divided
½ cup oil
2 packages (8 ounces
   each) PHILADELPHIA®
   Cream Cheese,
   softened
1 container (8 ounces)
   BREAKSTONE'S® or
   KNUDSEN® Sour Cream
½ cup granulated sugar
1 teaspoon grated lemon
   peel
1 tablespoon lemon juice
   Powdered sugar

MIX cake mix, 1 egg and oil. Press mixture onto bottom and up sides of lightly greased 15×10×1-inch baking pan. Bake at 350°F for 10 minutes.

BEAT cream cheese with electric mixer on medium speed until smooth. Add remaining 2 eggs, sour cream, granulated sugar, peel and juice; mix until blended. Pour batter into crust.

BAKE at 350°F for 30 to 35 minutes or until filling is just set in center and edges are light golden brown. Cool. Sprinkle with powdered sugar. Cut into bars. Store leftover bars in refrigerator.   *Makes 2 dozen*

Prep Time: 15 minutes
Bake Time: 35 minutes

Swiss Chocolate Crispies

1 package DUNCAN HINES®
   Moist Deluxe® Swiss
   Chocolate Cake Mix
½ cup shortening plus
   additional for greasing
½ cup butter or margarine,
   softened
2 eggs
2 tablespoons water
3 cups crispy rice cereal,
   divided

1. Combine cake mix, ½ cup shortening, butter, eggs and water in large bowl. Beat at low speed with electric mixer for 2 minutes. Fold in 1 cup cereal. Refrigerate 1 hour.

2. Crush remaining 2 cups cereal into coarse crumbs.

3. Preheat oven to 350°F. Grease cookie sheets. Shape dough into 1-inch balls. Roll in crushed cereal. Place on cookie sheets about 1 inch apart.

4. Bake 11 to 13 minutes. Cool 1 minute on cookie sheets. Remove to wire racks.

Makes about 4 dozen cookies

Creamy Lemon Bars

Quick-Fix Gingersnaps

1 package (1 pound
  1.5 ounces) sugar
  cookie mix
½ cup (1 stick) butter or
  margarine, melted
1 egg
1 tablespoon light
  molasses
1 teaspoon ground ginger
½ teaspoon ground
  cinnamon
¼ cup sugar
½ cup finely chopped
  pecans

Preheat oven to 375°F.

Combine cookie mix, butter, egg, molasses, ginger and cinnamon in large bowl; mix well. Form dough into 1-inch balls. (Dampen hands when handling dough to prevent sticking.)

Place sugar in shallow bowl. Roll balls of dough in sugar to coat completely. Arrange 2 inches apart on ungreased cookie sheets; flatten slightly with back of metal spatula. Sprinkle with pecans.

Bake 8 to 10 minutes or until lightly browned. Cool 1 minute on cookie sheets. Transfer to wire racks and cool completely. Store in airtight container.

Makes about 4 dozen cookies

Buckeye Cookie Bars

1 (18¼-ounce) package
  chocolate cake mix
¼ cup vegetable oil
1 egg
1 cup chopped peanuts
1 (14-ounce) can EAGLE®
  BRAND Sweetened
  Condensed Milk (NOT
  evaporated milk)
½ cup peanut butter

1. Preheat oven to 350°F. In large mixing bowl, combine cake mix, oil and egg; beat at medium speed until crumbly. Stir in peanuts. Reserve 1½ cups crumb mixture; press remaining crumb mixture firmly on bottom of greased 13×9-inch baking pan.

2. In medium bowl, beat Eagle Brand with peanut butter until smooth; spread over prepared crust. Sprinkle with reserved crumb mixture.

3. Bake 25 to 30 minutes or until set. Cool. Cut into bars. Store loosely covered at room temperature.

Makes 24 to 36 bars

Prep Time: 20 minutes
Bake Time: 25 to 30 minutes

Quick-Fix Gingersnaps

Pumpkin Snack Bars

CAKE

- 1 package (2-layer size) spice cake mix
- 1 can (16 ounces) pumpkin
- ¾ cup MIRACLE WHIP® *or* MIRACLE WHIP® LIGHT Dressing
- 3 eggs

FROSTING

- 3½ cups powdered sugar
- ½ cup (1 stick) butter *or* margarine, softened
- 2 tablespoons milk
- 1 teaspoon vanilla

CAKE

BLEND cake mix, pumpkin, dressing and eggs with electric mixer on medium speed until well blended. Pour into greased 15×10×1-inch baking pan.

BAKE at 350°F for 18 to 20 minutes or until toothpick inserted in center comes out clean. Cool completely on wire rack.

FROSTING

BLEND all ingredients with electric mixer on low speed until moistened. Beat on high speed until light and fluffy. Spread over cake. Cut into bars.

Makes about 3 dozen bars

Note: Bars can be baked in greased 13×9-inch baking pan. Bake at 350°F for 32 to 35 minutes or until toothpick inserted in center comes out clean. Cool and frost as directed.

Prep Time: 20 minutes
Bake Time: 20 minutes

Snickerdoodles

3 tablespoons sugar

1 teaspoon ground cinnamon

1 package DUNCAN HINES® Moist Deluxe® Classic Yellow Cake Mix

2 eggs

¼ cup vegetable oil

1. Preheat oven to 375°F. Grease cookie sheets. Place sheets of foil on countertop for cooling cookies.

2. Combine sugar and cinnamon in small bowl.

3. Combine cake mix, eggs and oil in large bowl. Stir until well blended. Shape dough into 1-inch balls. Roll in cinnamon-sugar mixture. Place balls 2 inches apart on cookie sheets. Flatten balls with bottom of glass.

4. Bake at 375°F for 8 to 9 minutes or until set. Cool one minute on cookie sheets. Remove to foil to cool completely.   *Makes about 3 dozen cookies*

• Magical Tip •

When baking more than one sheet of cookies at a time, rotate the cookie sheets from front to back and top to bottom halfway through the baking time. This will ensure more even browning. Once the cookies are done and removed from the cookie sheets, let the cookie sheets cool to room temperature before placing more dough on them. Placing dough on warm cookie sheets can cause it to melt and spread—this may cause the cookies to have a different shape and texture, and they may also become overdone on the bottom before the inside is done.

Crispy Thumbprint Cookies

1 package (18.25 ounces)
   yellow cake mix
½ cup vegetable oil
¼ cup water
1 egg
3 cups crisp rice cereal,
   crushed
½ cup chopped walnuts
6 tablespoons raspberry or
   strawberry preserves

1. Preheat oven to 375°F.

2. Combine cake mix, oil, water and egg. Beat at medium speed of electric mixer until well blended. Add cereal and walnuts; mix until well blended.

3. Drop by heaping teaspoonfuls about 2 inches apart onto ungreased baking sheets. Use thumb to make indentation in each cookie. Spoon about ½ teaspoon preserves into center of each cookie.

4. Bake 9 to 11 minutes or until golden brown. Cool cookies 1 minute on baking sheet; remove from baking sheet to wire rack to cool completely.

Makes 3 dozen cookies

Chocolate Macaroon Squares

1 package (18.25 ounces)
   chocolate cake mix
⅓ cup butter or margarine,
   softened
1 large egg, lightly beaten
1 can (14 ounces) NESTLÉ®
   CARNATION Sweetened
   Condensed Milk
1 large egg
1 teaspoon vanilla extract
1⅓ cups flaked sweetened
   coconut, divided
1 cup chopped pecans
1 cup (6 ounces) NESTLÉ®
   TOLL HOUSE®
   Semi-Sweet
   Chocolate Morsels

PREHEAT oven to 350°F.

COMBINE cake mix, butter and egg in large bowl, mix with fork until crumbly. Press onto bottom of ungreased 13×9-inch baking pan. Combine sweetened condensed milk, egg and vanilla extract in medium bowl; beat until well blended. Stir in *1 cup* coconut, nuts and morsels.

SPREAD mixture evenly over base; sprinkle with *remaining* coconut. Bake for 28 to 30 minutes or until center is almost set (center will firm when cool). Cool in pan on wire rack.

Makes 24 squares

Crispy Thumbprint Cookies

Chocolate Caramel Nut Bars

1 package (18¼ ounces)
    devil's food cake mix
¾ cup butter, melted
½ cup milk, divided
60 vanilla caramels
1 cup cashews, coarsely
    chopped
1 cup semisweet chocolate
    chips

Preheat oven to 350°F. Grease 13×9-inch baking pan. Combine cake mix, butter and ¼ cup milk in medium bowl; mix well. Press half of batter into bottom of prepared pan.

Bake 7 to 8 minutes or until batter just begins to form crust. Remove from oven.

Meanwhile, combine caramels and remaining ¼ cup milk in heavy medium saucepan. Cook over low heat, stirring often, about 5 minutes or until caramels are melted and mixture is smooth.

Pour melted caramel mixture over partially baked crust. Combine cashews and chocolate chips in small bowl; sprinkle over caramel mixture.

Drop spoonfuls of remaining batter evenly over nut mixture. Return pan to oven; bake 18 to 20 minutes more or until top cake layer springs back when lightly touched. (Caramel center will be soft.) Let cool on wire rack before cutting into squares or bars. (Bars can be frozen; let thaw 20 to 25 minutes before serving.)

Makes about 48 bars

Chocolate Caramel Nut Bars

Dish: Bar Cookies — Recipe   Serves:

Chocolate - Caramel-Nut Bars
1 package (18¼ ounces) devils food cake mix
¾ cup butter or margarine, melted
½ cup milk, divided
60 vanilla caramels
1 cup cashew pieces, coarsely chopped
1 cup semisweet chocolate chips

PREHEAT oven to 350°F. Grease 13x9-inch ba
Combine cake mix, butter and ¼ cup milk in m

Strawberry Streusel Squares

1 package (about
    18 ounces) yellow
    cake mix, divided

3 tablespoons uncooked
    old-fashioned oats

1 tablespoon margarine

1½ cups sliced strawberries

¾ cup plus 2 tablespoons
    water, divided

¾ cup diced strawberries

3 egg whites

⅓ cup unsweetened
    applesauce

½ teaspoon ground
    cinnamon

⅛ teaspoon ground nutmeg

1. Preheat oven to 350°F. Spray 13×9-inch baking pan with nonstick cooking spray; lightly coat with flour.

2. Combine ½ cup cake mix and oats in small bowl. Cut in margarine until mixture resembles coarse crumbs; set aside.

3. Place 1½ cups sliced strawberries and 2 tablespoons water in blender or food processor. Process until smooth. Transfer to small bowl and stir in ¾ cup diced strawberries. Set aside.

4. Place remaining cake mix in large bowl. Add ¾ cup water, egg whites, applesauce, cinnamon and nutmeg. Blend 30 seconds at low speed or just until moistened. Beat at medium speed 2 minutes. Pour batter into prepared pan.

5. Spoon strawberry mixture evenly over batter, spreading lightly. Sprinkle evenly with oat mixture. Bake 31 to 34 minutes or until wooden toothpick inserted into center comes out clean. Cool completely in pan on wire rack. *Makes 12 servings*

Banana Gingerbread Bars

1 package (14.5 ounces)
    gingerbread cake mix
½ cup lukewarm water
1 ripe, medium DOLE®
    Banana, mashed
    (about ½ cup)
1 egg
1 small DOLE® Banana,
    peeled and chopped
½ cup DOLE® Seedless
    Raisins
½ cup slivered almonds
1½ cups powdered sugar
    Juice from 1 lemon

• Preheat oven to 350°F.

• In large mixer bowl, combine gingerbread mix, water, banana purée and egg. Beat on low speed of electric mixer 1 minute.

• Stir in chopped banana, raisins and almonds.

• Spread batter in greased 13×9-inch baking pan. Bake 20 to 25 minutes or until top springs back when lightly touched.

• In medium bowl, mix powdered sugar and 3 tablespoons lemon juice to make thin glaze. Spread over warm gingerbread. Cool before cutting into bars. Sprinkle with additional powdered sugar, if desired.

Makes about 32 bars

Magical Tip

If your powdered sugar has lumps, it is helpful to sift it before using to make sure the glaze or any recipe it will be used in turns out smooth. Another way to sift powdered sugar is to place it in a food processor and process until light. (Always measure out the sugar before sifting unless the recipe calls for sifted powdered sugar.)

Chocolate Chip 'n Oatmeal Cookies

1 package (18.25 or
    18.5 ounces) yellow
    cake mix
1 cup quick-cooking rolled
    oats, uncooked
¾ cup butter or margarine,
    softened
2 eggs
1 cup HERSHEY'S Semi-
    Sweet Chocolate Chips

1. Heat oven to 350°F.

2. Combine cake mix, oats, butter and eggs in large bowl; mix well. Stir in chocolate chips. Drop by rounded teaspoons onto ungreased cookie sheets.

3. Bake 10 to 12 minutes or until very lightly browned. Cool slightly; remove from cookie sheets to wire racks. Cool completely.   *Makes about 4 dozen cookies*

Coconut Clouds

2⅔ cups flaked coconut,
    divided
1 package DUNCAN HINES®
    Moist Deluxe® Classic
    Yellow Cake Mix
1 egg
½ cup vegetable oil
¼ cup water
1 teaspoon almond extract

1. Preheat oven to 350°F. Place 1⅓ cups coconut in medium bowl; set aside.

2. Combine cake mix, egg, oil, water and almond extract in large bowl. Beat at low speed with electric mixer. Stir in remaining 1⅓ cups coconut. Drop rounded teaspoonful dough into reserved coconut. Roll to cover lightly. Place on ungreased baking sheet. Repeat with remaining dough, placing balls 2 inches apart. Bake at 350°F 10 to 12 minutes or until light golden brown. Cool 1 minute on baking sheets. Remove to cooling racks. Cool completely. Store in airtight container.   *Makes 3½ dozen cookies*

Cook's Note: To save time when forming dough into balls, use a 1-inch spring-operated cookie scoop. Spring-operated cookie scoops are available at kitchen specialty shops.

Chocolate Chip 'n Oatmeal Cookies

Chocolate Almond Biscotti

1 package DUNCAN HINES®
  Moist Deluxe® Dark
  Chocolate Cake Mix
1 cup all-purpose flour
½ cup (1 stick) butter or
  margarine, melted
2 eggs
1 teaspoon almond extract
½ cup chopped almonds
  White chocolate, melted
  (optional)

Preheat oven to 350°F. Line 2 baking sheets with parchment paper.

Combine cake mix, flour, butter, eggs and almond extract in large bowl. Beat at low speed with electric mixer until well blended; stir in nuts. Divide dough in half. Shape each half into a 12×2-inch log; place logs on prepared baking sheets. (Bake logs separately.)

Bake 30 to 35 minutes or until toothpick inserted in center comes out clean. Remove logs from oven; cool on baking sheets 15 minutes. Using serrated knife, cut logs into ½-inch slices. Arrange slices on baking sheets. Bake biscotti 10 minutes. Remove to cooling racks; cool completely.

Dip one end of each biscotti in melted white chocolate, if desired. Allow white chocolate to set at room temperature before storing biscotti in airtight container.

Makes about 2½ dozen cookies

Chocolate Almond Biscotti

Express

Chocolate Pudding Poke Cake

1 package (2-layer size)
    white cake mix
2 egg whites
1 ⅓ cups water
4 cups cold fat free milk
2 packages (4-serving size
    each) JELL-O®
    Chocolate Flavor
    Fat Free Sugar Free
    Instant Reduced
    Calorie Pudding
    & Pie Filling

PREPARE and bake cake as directed on package for 13×9-inch baking pan using 2 egg whites and 1 ⅓ cup water. Remove from oven. Immediately poke holes down through cake to pan with round handle of a wooden spoon. (Or poke holes with a plastic drinking straw, using turning motion to make large holes.) Holes should be at 1-inch intervals.

POUR milk into large bowl. Add pudding mixes. Beat with wire whisk 2 minutes. Quickly pour about ½ of the thin pudding mixture evenly over warm cake and into holes to make stripes. Let remaining pudding mixture stand to thicken slightly. Spoon over top of cake, swirling to "frost" cake.

REFRIGERATE at least 1 hour or until ready to serve. Store cake in refrigerator. *Makes 15 servings*

Prep Time: 30 minutes plus refrigerating

Chocolate Pudding Poke Cake

Double Chocolate Chewies

1 package DUNCAN HINES®
Moist Deluxe® Butter
Recipe Fudge Cake Mix

2 eggs

½ cup butter or margarine,
melted

1 package (6 ounces) semi-
sweet chocolate chips

1 cup chopped nuts
Confectioners' sugar
(optional)

1. Preheat oven to 350°F. Grease 13×9×2-inch pan.

2. Combine cake mix, eggs and melted butter in large bowl. Stir until thoroughly blended. (Mixture will be stiff.) Stir in chocolate chips and nuts. Press mixture evenly in greased pan. Bake 25 to 30 minutes or until toothpick inserted in center comes out clean. *Do not overbake.* Cool completely. Cut into bars. Dust with confectioners' sugar, if desired.   *Makes 36 bars*

Tip: For a special effect, cut a paper towel into ¼-inch-wide strips. Place strips in diagonal pattern on top of cooled bars before cutting. Place confectioners' sugar in tea strainer. Tap strainer lightly to dust surface with sugar. Carefully remove strips.

Devil's Food Fudge Cookies

1 package DUNCAN HINES®
Moist Deluxe® Devil's
Food Cake Mix

2 eggs

½ cup vegetable oil

1 cup semisweet chocolate
chips

½ cup chopped walnuts

1. Preheat oven to 350°F. Grease baking sheets.

2. Combine cake mix, eggs and oil in large bowl. Stir until thoroughly blended. Stir in chocolate chips and walnuts. (Mixture will be stiff.) Shape dough into 36 (1¼-inch) balls. Place 2 inches apart on prepared baking sheets.

3. Bake at 350°F for 10 to 11 minutes. (Cookies will look moist.) *Do not overbake.* Cool 2 minutes on baking sheets. Remove to cooling racks. Cool completely. Store in airtight container.   *Makes 3 dozen cookies*

Tip: For a delicious flavor treat, substitute peanut butter chips for the chocolate chips and chopped peanuts for the chopped walnuts.

Double Chocolate Chewies

Fudgy Oatmeal Butterscotch Cookies

1 package (18.25 ounces) devil's food cake mix

1½ cups quick-cooking or old-fashioned oats, uncooked

¾ cup (1½ sticks) butter, melted

2 large eggs

1 tablespoon vegetable oil

1 teaspoon vanilla extract

1¼ cups "M&M's"® Chocolate Mini Baking Bits

1 cup butterscotch chips

Preheat oven to 350°F. In large bowl combine cake mix, oats, butter, eggs, oil and vanilla until well blended. Stir in "M&M's"® Chocolate Mini Baking Bits and butterscotch chips. Drop by heaping tablespoonfuls about 2 inches apart onto ungreased cookie sheets. Bake 10 to 12 minutes. Cool 1 minute on cookie sheets; cool completely on wire racks. Store in tightly covered container. *Makes about 3 dozen cookies*

Double Chocolate Fantasy Bars

1 (18¼-ounce) package chocolate cake mix

¼ cup vegetable oil

1 egg

1 cup chopped nuts

1 (14-ounce) can EAGLE® BRAND Sweetened Condensed Milk (NOT evaporated milk)

1 (6-ounce) package semi-sweet chocolate chips

1 teaspoon vanilla extract
Dash salt

1. Preheat oven to 350°F. Grease 13×9-inch baking pan. In large bowl, combine cake mix, oil and egg; beat at medium speed until crumbly. Stir in nuts. Reserve 1½ cups crumb mixture. Press remaining crumb mixture on bottom of prepared pan.

2. In small saucepan over medium heat, combine remaining ingredients. Cook and stir until chips melt.

3. Pour chocolate mixture evenly over prepared crust. Sprinkle reserved crumb mixture evenly over top. Bake 25 to 30 minutes or until set. Cool. Cut into bars. Store loosely covered at room temperature.

Makes 36 bars

Prep Time: 15 minutes
Bake Time: 25 to 30 minutes

Midnight Bliss Cake

1 package (2-layer size)
chocolate cake mix,
any variety

4 eggs

1 container (8 ounces)
BREAKSTONE'S® *or*
KNUDSEN Sour Cream

½ cup GENERAL FOODS
INTERNATIONAL
COFFEES®, any flavor

1 package (4-serving size)
JELL-O® Chocolate
Flavor Instant Pudding
& Pie Filling

½ cup oil

½ cup water

1 package (8 squares)
BAKER'S® Semi-Sweet
Baking Chocolate,
chopped

HEAT oven to 350°F. Lightly grease and flour 12-cup fluted tube pan or 10-inch tube pan.

BEAT all ingredients except chopped chocolate in large bowl with electric mixer on low speed just until moistened, scraping side of bowl often. Beat on medium speed 2 minutes or until well blended. Stir in chopped chocolate. Pour into prepared pan.

BAKE 50 to 60 minutes or until toothpick inserted near center comes out clean. Cool in pan 10 minutes on wire rack. Loosen cake from sides of pan with small knife or spatula. Invert cake onto rack; gently remove pan. Cool completely on wire rack. Sprinkle with powdered sugar, if desired.   *Makes 12 to 16 servings*

Great Substitute: Substitute 2 tablespoons MAXWELL HOUSE® Instant Coffee for ½ cup GENERAL FOODS INTERNATIONAL COFFEES®.

Prep Time: 15 minutes
Bake Time: 60 minutes

Magical Tip

Since both heat and moisture adversely affect chocolate, it should be stored at room temperature wrapped in foil or waxed paper, but not plastic wrap. When chocolate is stored at too high a temperature, white or grey streaks or mottling appears on the surface (bloom). The bloom will not affect the chocolate's taste or baking quality.

Chocolate Petits Fours

1 package DUNCAN HINES®
Moist Deluxe® Dark
Chocolate Fudge Cake
Mix

1 package (7 ounces) pure
almond paste

½ cup seedless red
raspberry jam

3 cups semisweet chocolate
chips

½ cup plus 1 tablespoon
vegetable shortening
plus additional for
greasing

1. Preheat oven to 350°F. Grease and flour 13×9×2-inch pan.

2. Prepare, bake and cool cake following package directions for basic recipe. Remove from pan. Cover and store overnight (see Tip). Level top of cake. Trim ¼-inch strip of cake from all sides. (Be careful to make straight cuts.) Cut cake into small squares, rectangles or triangles with serrated knife. Cut round and heart shapes with 1½- to 2-inch cookie cutters. Split each individual cake horizontally into two layers.

3. For filling, cut almond paste in half. Roll half the paste between two sheets of waxed paper to ⅛-inch thickness. Cut into same shapes as individual cakes. Repeat with second half of paste. Warm jam in small saucepan over low heat until thin. Remove top of one cake. Spread ¼ to ½ teaspoon jam on inside of each cut surface. Place one almond paste cutout on bottom layer. Top with second half of cake, jam side down. Repeat with remaining cakes.

4. For glaze, place chocolate chips and ½ cup shortening in 4-cup glass measuring cup. Microwave at MEDIUM (50% power) for 2 minutes; stir. Microwave for 2 minutes longer at MEDIUM; stir until smooth. Place 3 assembled cakes on cooling rack over bowl. Spoon chocolate glaze over each cake until top and sides are completely covered. Remove to waxed paper when glaze has stopped dripping. Repeat process until all cakes are covered. (Return chocolate glaze in bowl to glass measuring cup as needed; microwave at MEDIUM for 30 to 60 seconds to thin.)

continued on page 86

Chocolate Petits Fours

Chocolate Petits Fours, continued

5. Place remaining chocolate glaze in resealable plastic bag; seal. Place bag in bowl of hot water for several minutes. Dry with paper towel. Knead until chocolate is smooth. Snip pinpoint hole in bottom corner of bag. Drizzle or decorate top of each petit four. Let stand until chocolate is set. Store in single layer in airtight containers. *Makes 24 to 32 servings*

Tip: To make cutting the cake into shapes easier, bake the cake one day before assembling.

Festive Fudge Blossoms

¼ cup butter, softened
1 box (18.25 ounces) chocolate fudge cake mix
1 egg, slightly beaten
2 tablespoons water
¾ to 1 cup finely chopped walnuts
48 chocolate star candies

1. Preheat oven to 350°F. Cut butter into cake mix in large bowl until mixture resembles coarse crumbs. Stir in egg and water until well blended.

2. Shape dough into ½-inch balls; roll in walnuts, pressing nuts gently into dough. Place about 2 inches apart on ungreased baking sheets.

3. Bake cookies 12 minutes or until puffed and nearly set. Place chocolate star in center of each cookie; bake 1 minute. Cool 2 minutes on baking sheets. Remove cookies from baking sheets to wire racks to cool completely. *Makes 4 dozen cookies*

Festive Fudge Blossoms

Double Chocolate Snack Cake

1 package DUNCAN HINES®
   Moist Deluxe® Devil's
   Food Cake Mix

1 cup white chocolate
   chips, divided

½ cup semisweet chocolate
   chips

Preheat oven to 350°F. Grease and flour 13×9-inch baking pan.

Prepare cake mix as directed on package. Stir in ½ cup white chocolate chips and semisweet chips. Pour into prepared pan. Bake 35 to 40 minutes or until toothpick inserted in center comes out clean. Remove from oven; sprinkle top with remaining ½ cup white chocolate chips. Serve warm or cool completely in pan.

Makes 12 to 16 servings

Tip: For a special dessert, serve cake warm with a scoop of vanilla ice cream or whipped cream garnished with chocolate chips.

Chocolate Cherry Torte

1 package DUNCAN HINES®
   Moist Deluxe® Devil's
   Food Cake Mix

1 can (21 ounces) cherry
   pie filling

¼ teaspoon almond extract

1 container (8 ounces)
   frozen whipped
   topping, thawed and
   divided

¼ cup toasted sliced
   almonds, for garnish
   (see Tip)

1. Preheat oven to 350°F. Grease and flour two 9-inch round cake pans.

2. Prepare, bake and cool cake following package directions for basic recipe. Combine cherry pie filling and almond extract in small bowl. Stir until blended.

3. To assemble, place one cake layer on serving plate. Spread with 1 cup whipped topping, then half the cherry pie filling mixture. Top with second cake layer. Spread remaining pie filling to within 1½ inches of cake edge. Decorate cake edge with remaining whipped topping. Garnish with sliced almonds.

Makes 12 to 16 servings

Tip: To toast almonds, spread in a single layer on baking sheet. Bake at 325°F 4 to 6 minutes or until fragrant and golden.

Double Chocolate Snack Cake

Easy Turtle Squares

1 package (about 18 ounces) chocolate cake mix

½ cup butter, melted

¼ cup milk

1 cup (6-ounce package) semisweet chocolate chips

1 cup chopped pecans, divided

1 jar (12 ounces) caramel ice cream topping

Preheat oven to 350°F. Spray 13×9-inch pan with nonstick cooking spray. Combine cake mix, butter and milk in large bowl. Press half of batter into prepared pan. Bake 7 to 8 minutes or until batter begins to form crust. Carefully remove from oven. Sprinkle chocolate chips and ½ cup pecans over partially baked crust. Drizzle caramel topping over chips and pecans. Drop spoonfuls of remaining cake batter over caramel mixture; sprinkle with remaining ½ cup pecans. Return to oven; bake 18 to 20 minutes longer or until top of cake layer springs back when lightly touched. (Caramel center will be soft.) Cool completely on wire rack. Cut into squares. *Makes 24 bar cookies*

Chocolate-Chocolate Cake

1 package (8 ounces) PHILADELPHIA® Cream Cheese, softened

1 cup BREAKSTONE'S® or KNUDSEN® Sour Cream

½ cup coffee-flavored liqueur or water

2 eggs

1 package (2-layer size) chocolate cake mix

1 package (4-serving size) JELL-O® Chocolate Flavor Instant Pudding & Pie Filling

1 cup BAKER'S® Semi-Sweet Real Chocolate Chips

MIX cream cheese, sour cream, liqueur and eggs with electric mixer on medium speed until well blended. Add cake mix and pudding mix; beat until well blended. Fold in chips. (Batter will be stiff.)

POUR into greased and floured 12-cup fluted tube pan.

BAKE at 325°F for 1 hour to 1 hour and 5 minutes or until toothpick inserted near center comes out clean. Cool 5 minutes. Remove from pan. Cool completely on wire rack. Sprinkle with powdered sugar before serving. Garnish, if desired. *Makes 10 to 12 servings*

Prep Time: 10 minutes plus cooling
Bake Time: 1 hour 5 minutes

Easy Turtle Squares

Enchanting
Desserts

Strawberry Shortcake

CAKE

1 package DUNCAN HINES®
   Moist Deluxe® French
   Vanilla Cake Mix

3 eggs

1¼ cups water

½ cup butter or margarine,
   softened

FILLING AND TOPPING

2 cups whipping cream,
   chilled

⅓ cup sugar

½ teaspoon vanilla extract

1 quart fresh strawberries,
   rinsed, drained and
   sliced

Mint leaves, for garnish

1. Preheat oven to 350°F. Grease two 9-inch round cake pans with butter or margarine. Sprinkle bottom and sides with granulated sugar.

2. For cake, combine cake mix, eggs, water and butter in large bowl. Beat at low speed with electric mixer until moistened. Beat at medium speed for 2 minutes. Pour into pans. Bake at 350°F 30 to 35 minutes or until toothpick inserted in center comes out clean. Cool in pan 10 minutes. Invert onto cooling rack. Cool completely.

3. For filling and topping, place whipping cream, sugar and vanilla extract in large bowl. Beat with electric mixer on high speed until stiff peaks form. Reserve ⅓ cup for garnish. Place one cake layer on serving plate. Spread with half of whipped cream and half of sliced strawberries. Place second layer on top of strawberries. Spread with remaining whipping cream and top with remaining strawberries. Dollop with reserved ½ cup whipped cream and garnish with mint leaves. Refrigerate until ready to serve. *Makes 12 servings*

Strawberry Shortcake

Streusel Coffeecake

32 CHIPS AHOY!® Chocolate Chip Cookies, divided

1 (18- to 18.5-ounce) package yellow or white cake mix

½ cup BREAKSTONE'S® or KNUDSEN® Sour Cream

½ cup PLANTERS® Pecans, chopped

½ cup BAKER'S® ANGEL FLAKE® Coconut

¼ cup packed brown sugar

1 teaspoon ground cinnamon

⅓ cup margarine or butter, melted

Powdered sugar glaze, optional

1. Coarsely chop 20 cookies; finely crush remaining 12 cookies. Set aside.

2. Prepare cake mix batter according to package directions; blend in sour cream. Stir in chopped cookies. Pour batter into greased and floured 13×9×2-inch baking pan.

3. Mix cookie crumbs, pecans, coconut, brown sugar and cinnamon; stir in margarine or butter. Sprinkle over cake batter.

4. Bake at 350°F for 40 minutes or until toothpick inserted in center of cake comes out clean. Cool completely. Drizzle with powdered sugar glaze if desired. Cut into squares to serve.

Makes 24 servings

Prep Time: 25 minutes
Bake Time: 40 minutes

Fudge Rum Balls

1 package DUNCAN HINES® Moist Deluxe® Butter Recipe Fudge Cake Mix

1 cup finely chopped pecans or walnuts

1 tablespoon rum extract

2 cups sifted confectioners' sugar

¼ cup unsweetened cocoa powder

Pecans or walnuts, finely chopped

1. Preheat oven to 375°F. Grease and flour 13×9×2-inch baking pan. Prepare, bake and cool cake following package directions.

2. Crumble cake into large bowl. Stir with fork until crumbs are fine and uniform in size. Add 1 cup nuts, rum extract, confectioners' sugar and cocoa. Stir until well blended.

3. Shape heaping tablespoonfuls of mixture into balls. Garnish by rolling balls in finely chopped nuts. Press firmly to adhere nuts to balls.

Makes 6 dozen

Streusel Coffeecake

Banana Brunch Coffee Cake

2 ripe, medium DOLE®
   Bananas

1 package (18.25 ounces)
   yellow cake mix

1 package (3.4 ounces)
   instant vanilla pudding
   mix (4 servings)

½ cup vegetable oil

4 eggs

1 teaspoon vanilla extract

½ cup chopped almonds

⅓ cup packed brown sugar

1 teaspoon ground
   cinnamon

½ teaspoon ground nutmeg

• Purée bananas in blender, (1 cup). Combine bananas, cake mix, pudding mix, oil, eggs and vanilla in large mixing bowl. Mix well and beat at medium speed 8 minutes, scraping side of bowl occasionally.

• Combine almonds, brown sugar, cinnamon and nutmeg. Pour one-half cake batter into greased 3-quart Bundt pan. Sprinkle with almond mixture. Cover with remaining batter. Insert knife in batter and swirl in figure eight patterns through layers. (Be sure not to overmix layers.)

• Bake at 300°F 55 to 60 minutes. Cool in pan on wire rack 10 minutes. Invert onto rack to complete cooling. Dust with powdered sugar when cool, if desired. Garnish with sliced bananas, raspberries and fresh mint, if desired. *Makes 12 servings*

Prep Time: 15 minutes
Bake Time: 60 minutes

Punch Bowl Party Cake

1 package (18¼ ounces)
    yellow cake mix plus
    ingredients to prepare
    mix
1 package (4-serving size)
    vanilla flavor instant
    pudding and pie filling
    mix plus ingredients to
    prepare mix
2 cans (21 ounces each)
    cherry pie filling
1 cup chopped pecans
1 container (12 ounces)
    frozen nondairy
    whipped topping,
    thawed

1. Prepare cake mix and bake according to package directions for 13×9-inch cake; cool completely.

2. Prepare pudding mix according to package directions.

3. Crumble ½ of cake into bottom of small punch bowl. Cover with ½ of pudding.

4. Reserve a few cherries from one can of cherry pie filling for garnish. Top pudding with layers of cherry pie filling, nuts and whipped topping.

5. Repeat layers, using remaining cake, pudding and cherry pie filling. Top with remaining nuts and whipped topping. Garnish with reserved cherries.

Makes one cake

Enchanting Desserts

Magical Tip

Purchase nuts in small quantities, as they have a high fat content and can quickly become rancid. Store nuts in an airtight container in a cool place, and always taste them before using to make sure they are still good.

Decadent Chocolate Delight

1 package chocolate
    cake mix
8 ounces sour cream
1 cup chocolate chips
1 cup water
4 eggs
¾ cup vegetable oil
1 package (4-serving size)
    chocolate flavor
    instant pudding and
    pie filling mix

SLOW COOKER DIRECTIONS
Lightly grease inside of slow cooker.

Combine all ingredients in large bowl. Pour into slow cooker. Cover and cook on LOW 6 to 8 hours or on HIGH 3 to 4 hours. Serve hot or warm with ice cream.

Makes 12 servings

Saucy Bake

1 package (2-layer size)
    yellow or devil's food
    cake mix or cake mix
    with pudding in the
    mix
2 cups water
2 cups milk
2 packages (4-serving size)
    JELL-O® Chocolate
    Flavor Instant Pudding
    & Pie Filling
⅓ cup sugar
¼ to ½ teaspoon ground
    cinnamon

HEAT oven to 350°F.

PREPARE cake mix as directed on package. Pour batter into greased 13×9-inch baking pan. Pour water and milk into large bowl. Add pudding mixes, sugar and cinnamon. Beat with electric mixer on low speed 1 to 2 minutes or until well blended. Pour over cake batter in pan.

BAKE 1 hour or until cake tester inserted in center comes out clean. Garnish as desired. Serve warm.

Makes 15 servings

Prep Time: 30 minutes
Bake Time: 1 hour

Decadent Chocolate Delight

Lemon Poppy Seed Cupcakes

CUPCAKES

1 package DUNCAN HINES®
    Moist Deluxe® Lemon
    Supreme Cake Mix

3 eggs

1⅓ cups water

⅓ cup vegetable oil

3 tablespoons poppy seed

LEMON FROSTING

1 container (16 ounces)
    DUNCAN HINES®
    Vanilla Frosting

1 teaspoon grated lemon
    peel

¼ teaspoon lemon extract

3 to 4 drops yellow food
    coloring

Yellow and orange
    gumdrops, for garnish

1. Preheat oven to 350°F. Place 30 (2½-inch) paper liners in muffin cups.

2. For cupcakes, combine cake mix, eggs, water, oil and poppy seed in large bowl. Beat at medium speed of electric mixer 2 minutes. Fill paper liners about half full. Bake 18 to 21 minutes or until toothpick inserted in center comes out clean. Cool in pans 5 minutes. Remove to cooling racks. Cool completely.

3. For lemon frosting, combine Vanilla frosting, lemon peel and lemon extract in small bowl. Tint with yellow food coloring to desired color. Frost cupcakes with lemon frosting. Decorate with gumdrops.

Makes 30 cupcakes

Lemon Poppy Seed Cupcakes

Apple-Gingerbread Mini Cakes

Enchanting Desserts

1 large Cortland or
    Jonathan apple, cored
    and quartered
1 package (14½ ounces)
    gingerbread cake
    and cookie mix
1 cup water
1 egg
    Powdered sugar

1. Lightly grease 10 (6- to 7-ounce) custard cups; set aside. Grate apple in food processor or with hand-held grater. Combine grated apple, cake mix, water and egg in medium bowl; stir until well blended. Spoon about ⅓ cup mix into each custard cup, filling cups half full.

2. Arrange 5 cups in microwave. Microwave at HIGH 2 minutes. Rotate cups ½ turn. Microwave 1 minute more or until cakes are springy when touched and look slightly moist on top. Cool on wire rack. Repeat with remaining cakes.

3. To unmold cakes, run a small knife around edge of custard cups to loosen cakes while still warm. Invert on cutting board and tap lightly until cakes drop out. Place on plates. When cool enough, dust with powdered sugar, if desired. Serve warm or at room temperature.

Makes 10 cakes

Serving Suggestion: Serve with vanilla ice cream, whipped cream or crème anglaise.

Magical Tip

Cortland and Jonathan are both all-purpose apple varieties, good for both cooking and eating raw. Apples should be stored in a cool, dry place or refrigerated in a plastic bag. Apples in good condition can last up to six weeks in the refrigerator.

Apple-Gingerbread Mini Cakes

Individual Cheesecake Cups

CRUST

 1 package DUNCAN HINES®
 Moist Deluxe® Classic
 Yellow or Devil's Food
 Cake Mix

 ¼ cup margarine or butter,
 melted

CHEESE FILLING

 2 packages (8 ounces
 each) cream cheese,
 softened

 3 eggs

 ¾ cup sugar

 1 teaspoon vanilla extract

TOPPING

 1½ cups dairy sour cream

 ¼ cup sugar

 1 can (21 ounces) cherry
 pie filling (optional)

1. Preheat oven to 350°F. Place 2½-inch foil or paper liners in 24 muffin cups.

2. For crust, combine cake mix and melted ¼ cup margarine in large bowl. Beat at low speed with electric mixer for 1 minute. Mixture will be crumbly. Divide mixture evenly among muffin cups. Level but do not press.

3. For filling, combine cream cheese, eggs, ¾ cup sugar and vanilla extract in medium bowl. Beat at medium speed with electric mixer until smooth. Spoon evenly into muffin cups. Bake at 350°F for 20 minutes or until set.

4. For topping, combine sour cream and ¼ cup sugar in small bowl. Spoon evenly over cheesecakes. Return to oven for 5 minutes. Cool completely. Garnish each cheesecake with cherry pie filling, if desired. Refrigerate until ready to serve. *Makes 24 servings*

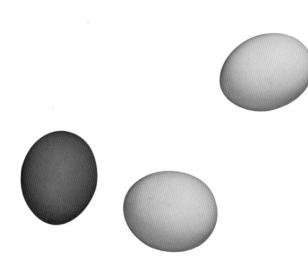

Raspberry Crumb Coffee Cake

COFFEE CAKE

- 1 (18.25-ounce) package deluxe white cake mix
- 1 cup all-purpose flour
- 1 package (¼-ounce) active dry yeast
- ⅔ cup warm water
- 2 eggs
- 1½ cups (18-ounce jar) SMUCKER'S® Red Raspberry Preserves
- ¼ cup sugar
- 1 teaspoon cinnamon
- 6 tablespoons butter or margarine

TOPPING

- 1 cup powdered sugar
- 1 tablespoon corn syrup
- 1 to 3 tablespoons milk

Grease 13×9-inch pan. Reserve 2½ cups dry cake mix. Combine remaining cake mix, flour, yeast, water and eggs. Mix by hand 100 strokes. Spread batter in greased pan. Spoon preserves evenly over batter.

Combine reserved cake mix, sugar and cinnamon; cut in butter with fork until fine particles form. Sprinkle over preserves.

Bake at 375°F for 30 to 35 minutes or until golden brown.

Combine all topping ingredients, adding enough milk for desired drizzling consistency. Drizzle over warm or cooled coffee cake.   *Makes 12 to 16 servings*

Magical Tip

To make sure the powdered sugar topping is perfectly smooth, sift the powdered sugar before combining it with the other ingredients. (But sift it *after* measuring.) Let the cake cool at least 10 minutes before drizzling with the glaze, or else the glaze will melt into the top of the cake.

Brownie Ice Cream Pie

1 (21-ounce) package
   DUNCAN HINES® Chewy
   Fudge Brownie Mix
2 eggs
½ cup vegetable oil
¼ cup water
¾ cup semisweet chocolate
   chips
1 (9-inch) unbaked pastry
   crust
1 (10-ounce) package
   frozen sweetened
   sliced strawberries
   Vanilla ice cream

Preheat oven to 350°F.

Combine brownie mix, eggs, oil and water in large bowl. Stir with spoon until well blended, about 50 strokes. Stir in chips. Spoon into crust. Bake 40 to 45 minutes or until set. Cool completely. Purée strawberries in food processor or blender. Cut pie into wedges. Serve with ice cream and puréed strawberries.

Makes 8 servings

Golden Apple Cupcakes

1 package (18 to
   20 ounces) yellow
   cake mix
1 cup MOTT'S® Chunky
   Apple Sauce
⅓ cup vegetable oil
3 eggs
¼ cup firmly packed light
   brown sugar
¼ cup chopped walnuts
½ teaspoon ground
   cinnamon
   Vanilla Frosting (recipe
   follows)

Heat oven to 350°F. In bowl, combine cake mix, apple sauce, oil and eggs; blend according to package directions. Spoon batter into 24 paper-lined muffin pan cups. Mix brown sugar, walnuts and cinnamon; sprinkle over prepared batter in muffin cups. Bake 20 to 25 minutes or until toothpick inserted in center comes out clean. Cool in pan 10 minutes. Remove from pan; cool completely on wire rack. Frost cupcakes with Vanilla Frosting.

Makes 24 cupcakes

Vanilla Frosting: In large bowl, beat 1 package (8 ounces) softened cream cheese until light and creamy; blend in ¼ teaspoon vanilla extract. Beat ½ cup heavy cream until stiff; fold into cream cheese mixture.

Brownie Ice Cream Pie

Pumpkin Bread

1 package (about
    18 ounces) yellow
    cake mix
1 can (16 ounces) solid
    pack pumpkin
⅓ cup GRANDMA'S®
    Molasses
4 eggs
1 teaspoon cinnamon
1 teaspoon nutmeg
⅓ cup nuts, chopped
    (optional)
⅓ cup raisins (optional)

Preheat oven to 350°F. Grease two 9×5-inch loaf pans.

Combine all ingredients in a large bowl and mix well. Beat at medium speed 2 minutes. Pour into prepared pans. Bake 60 minutes or until toothpick inserted in center comes out clean. *Makes 2 loaves*

Hint: Serve with cream cheese or preserves, or top with cream cheese frosting or ice cream.

Cran-Lemon Coffee Cake

1 package (18.25 ounces)
    yellow cake mix with
    pudding in the mix
1 cup water
⅓ cup butter, melted and
    cooled
¼ cup fresh lemon juice
3 eggs
1 tablespoon grated lemon
    peel
1½ cups coarsely chopped
    cranberries

Preheat oven to 350°F. Grease and flour 12-inch tube pan. Beat cake mix, water, butter, lemon juice, eggs and lemon peel in large bowl with electric mixer on low speed 2 minutes. Fold in cranberries. Spread batter evenly in prepared pan.

Bake about 55 minutes or until wooden pick inserted in center comes out clean. Cool on wire rack 10 minutes. Remove from pan; cool on wire rack. Coffee cake may be served warm or at room temperature.

Makes 12 servings

Pumpkin Bread

Treats

Ice Cream Cone Cupcakes

1 package (18¼ ounces) white cake mix plus ingredients to prepare mix

2 tablespoons nonpareils*

2 packages flat-bottomed ice cream cones (about 24 cones total)

1 container (16 ounces) vanilla or chocolate frosting

Candies and other decorations

*Nonpareils are tiny, round, brightly colored sprinkles used for cake and cookie decorating.

1. Preheat oven to 350°F.

2. Prepare cake mix according to package directions. Stir in nonpareils.

3. Spoon ¼ cup batter into each ice cream cone.

4. Stand cones on cookie sheet. Bake cones until toothpick inserted into center of cake comes out clean, about 20 minutes. Cool on wire racks.

5. Frost each filled cone. Decorate as desired.

Makes 24 cupcakes

Note: Cupcakes are best served the day they are prepared. Store loosely covered.

Ice Cream Cone Cupcakes

Strawberry Stripe Refrigerator Cake

CAKE

1 package DUNCAN HINES®
   Moist Deluxe® Classic
   White Cake Mix

2 packages (10 ounces)
   frozen sweetened
   strawberry slices,
   thawed

TOPPING

1 package (4-serving)
   vanilla instant pudding
   and pie filling mix

1 cup milk

1 cup whipping cream,
   whipped

   Fresh strawberries, for
   garnish (optional)

1. Preheat oven to 350°F. Grease and flour 13×9×2-inch pan.

2. For cake, prepare, bake and cool following package directions. Poke holes 1 inch apart in top of cake using handle of wooden spoon. Purée thawed strawberries with juice in blender or food processor. Spoon evenly over top of cake, allowing mixture to soak into holes.

3. For topping, combine pudding mix and milk in large bowl. Stir until smooth. Fold in whipped cream. Spread over cake. Decorate with fresh strawberries, if desired. Refrigerate at least 4 hours. *Makes 12 to 16 servings*

Tip: For a Neapolitan Refrigerator Cake, replace the White Cake Mix with Duncan Hines® Moist Deluxe® Devil's Food Cake Mix and follow directions listed above.

Colorific Pizza Cookie

1 package (1 pound
   1.5 ounces) sugar
   cookie mix

²⁄₃ cup mini candy coated
   chocolate pieces

¹⁄₃ cup powdered sugar

2 to 3 teaspoons milk

Preheat oven to 375°F.

Prepare cookie mix according to package directions. Spread into ungreased 12-inch pizza pan. Sprinkle evenly with chocolate pieces; press gently into dough.

Bake 20 to 24 minutes or until lightly browned. Cool 2 minutes in pan. Transfer to wire rack and cool completely.

Blend powdered sugar and milk until smooth, adding enough milk to reach drizzling consistency. Drizzle icing over cooled pizza cookie with spoon or fork. Cut into wedges. *Makes 12 servings*

Strawberry Stripe Refrigerator Cake

Snowman Cupcakes

1 package (18.5 ounces) yellow or white cake mix plus ingredients to prepare mix

2 containers (16 ounces each) vanilla frosting

4 cups flaked coconut

15 large marshmallows

15 miniature chocolate covered peanut butter cups, unwrapped

Small red candies and pretzel sticks for decoration

Green and red decorating gel

Preheat oven to 350°F. Line 15 regular-size (2½-inch) muffin pan cups and 15 small (about 1-inch) muffin pan cups with paper muffin cup liners. Prepare cake mix according to package directions. Spoon batter into muffin cups.

Bake 10 to 15 minutes for small cupcakes and 15 to 20 minutes for large cupcakes or until cupcakes are golden and toothpick inserted into centers comes out clean. Cool in pans on wire racks 10 minutes. Remove from pans to racks; cool completely. Remove paper liners.

For each snowman, frost bottom and side of 1 large cupcake; coat with coconut. Repeat with 1 small cupcake. Attach small cupcake to large cupcake with frosting to form snowman body. Attach marshmallow to small cupcake with frosting to form snowman head. Attach inverted peanut butter cup to marshmallow with frosting to form snowman hat. Use pretzels for arms and small red candies for buttons as shown in photo. Pipe faces with decorating gel as shown. Repeat with remaining cupcakes.

Makes 15 snowmen

· Magical Tip ·

To easily fill muffin cups, place batter in a 4-cup glass measure. Pour batter into the muffin cups, filling each cup about ¾ full. Use a plastic spatula to control the flow of the batter.

Snowman Cupcakes

Fudgy Banana Oat Cake

TOPPING:

> 1 cup QUAKER® Oats (quick or old fashioned, uncooked)
>
> ½ cup firmly packed brown sugar
>
> ¼ cup (½ stick) margarine or butter, chilled

FILLING:

> 1 cup (6 ounces) semisweet chocolate pieces
>
> ⅔ cup sweetened condensed milk (not evaporated milk)
>
> 1 tablespoon margarine or butter

CAKE:

> 1 package (18.25 ounces) devil's food cake mix
>
> 1¼ cups mashed ripe bananas (about 3 large)
>
> ⅓ cup vegetable oil
>
> 3 eggs
>
> Banana slices (optional)
>
> Whipped cream (optional)

Heat oven to 350°F. Lightly grease bottom only of 13×9-inch baking pan. For topping, combine oats and brown sugar. Cut in margarine until mixture is crumbly; set aside.

For filling, in small saucepan, heat chocolate pieces, sweetened condensed milk and margarine over low heat until chocolate is melted, stirring occasionally. Remove from heat; set aside.

For cake, in large mixing bowl, combine cake mix, bananas, oil and eggs. Blend at low speed of electric mixer until dry ingredients are moistened. Beat at medium speed 2 minutes. Spread batter evenly into prepared pan. Drop chocolate mixture by teaspoonfuls evenly over batter. Sprinkle with reserved oat mixture. Bake 40 to 45 minutes or until cake pulls away from sides of pan and topping is golden brown. Cool cake in pan on wire rack. Garnish with banana slices and sweetened whipped cream, if desired.

Makes 15 servings

Ice Cream Cookie Sandwich

2 pints chocolate chip ice
  cream, softened
1 package DUNCAN HINES®
  Moist Deluxe® Dark
  Chocolate Fudge
  Cake Mix
½ cup butter or margarine,
  softened

1. Line bottom of one 9-inch round cake pan with aluminum foil. Spread ice cream in pan; return to freezer until firm. Run knife around edge of pan to loosen ice cream. Remove from pan; wrap in foil and return to freezer.

2. Preheat oven to 350°F. Line bottom of two 9-inch round cake pans with aluminum foil. Place cake mix in large bowl. Add butter; mix thoroughly until crumbs form. Place half the cake mix in each pan; press lightly. Bake 15 minutes or until browned around edges; do not overbake. Cool 10 minutes; remove from pans. Remove foil from cookie layers; cool completely.

3. To assemble, place one cookie layer on serving plate. Top with ice cream. Peel off foil. Place second cookie layer on top. Wrap in foil and freeze 2 hours. To keep longer, store in airtight container. Let stand at room temperature for 5 to 10 minutes before cutting.

Makes 10 to 12 servings

Kids' Confetti Cake

CAKE

- 1 package DUNCAN HINES® Moist Deluxe® Classic Yellow Cake Mix
- 1 package (4-serving size) vanilla instant pudding and pie filling mix
- 4 eggs
- 1 cup water
- ½ cup vegetable oil
- 1 cup semi-sweet mini chocolate chips

TOPPING

- 1 cup colored miniature marshmallows
- ⅔ cup DUNCAN HINES® Creamy Home-Style Chocolate Frosting
- 2 tablespoons semi-sweet mini chocolate chips

1. Preheat oven to 350°F. Grease and flour 13×9×2-inch baking pan.

2. For cake, combine cake mix, pudding mix, eggs, water and oil in large bowl. Beat at medium speed with electric mixer 2 minutes. Stir in 1 cup chocolate chips. Pour into pan. Bake 40 to 45 minutes or until toothpick inserted in center comes out clean.

3. For topping, immediately arrange marshmallows evenly over hot cake. Place frosting in microwave-safe bowl. Microwave at HIGH (100% power) 25 to 30 seconds. Stir until smooth. Drizzle evenly over marshmallows and cake. Sprinkle with 2 tablespoons chocolate chips. Cool completely.

Makes 12 to 16 servings

Magical Tip

Be sure to smell and taste your oil before cooking or baking with it, especially if you haven't used it in a while. Heat, light and time will turn oils rancid, and a rancid oil will ruin any dish it is used in. Oils should be stored in a cool, dark place; they will keep from three to six months. If a cool spot is not available, oils should be refrigerated.

Kids' Confetti Cake

Banana Split Cupcakes

1 (18.25 ounces) yellow cake mix, divided
1 cup water
1 cup mashed ripe bananas
3 eggs
1 cup chopped drained maraschino cherries
1½ cups miniature semi-sweet chocolate chips, divided
1½ cups prepared vanilla frosting
1 cup marshmallow creme
1 teaspoon shortening
30 whole maraschino cherries, drained and patted dry

1. Preheat oven to 350°F. Line 30 regular-size (2½-inch) muffin cups with paper muffin cup liners.

2. Reserve 2 tablespoons cake mix. Combine remaining cake mix, water, bananas and eggs in large bowl. Beat at low speed of electric mixer until moistened, about 30 seconds. Beat at medium speed 2 minutes. Combine chopped cherries and reserved cake mix in small bowl. Stir chopped cherry mixture and 1 cup chocolate chips into batter.

3. Spoon batter into prepared muffin cups. Bake 15 to 20 minutes or until toothpick inserted in centers comes out clean. Cool in pans on wire racks 10 minutes. Remove to wire racks; cool completely.

4. Combine frosting and marshmallow creme in medium bowl until well blended. Frost each cupcake with frosting mixture.

5. Combine remaining ½ cup chocolate chips and shortening in small microwavable bowl. Microwave at HIGH 30 to 45 seconds, stirring after 30 seconds, or until smooth. Drizzle chocolate mixture over cupcakes. Place one whole cherry on each cupcake.

Makes 30 cupcakes

Note: If desired, omit chocolate drizzle and top cupcakes with colored sprinkles.

Banana Split Cupcakes

Oreo® Pizza

14 Regular or Reduced Fat
    OREO® Chocolate
    Sandwich Cookies,
    chopped (about
    1 ½ cups)
1 (21-ounce) package
    brownie mix, batter
    prepared according to
    package directions
1 cup JET-PUFFED®
    Miniature
    Marshmallows
⅓ cup PLANTERS® Walnuts,
    chopped
⅓ cup candy-coated peanut
    butter candies

1. Stir cookie pieces into prepared brownie batter; spread in greased 14-inch pizza pan. Bake at 350°F for 18 to 20 minutes or until done.

2. Sprinkle marshmallows over top of hot brownie; bake for 2 to 3 minutes more or until marshmallows are puffed.

3. Sprinkle with nuts and candies, pressing lightly into softened marshmallows. Cool slightly on wire rack. Cut into wedges; serve warm or cooled.

Makes 8 servings

Marshmallow Krispie Bars

1 (21-ounce) package
    DUNCAN HINES®
    Family-Style Chewy
    Fudge Brownie Mix
1 package (10½ ounces)
    miniature
    marshmallows
1½ cups semi-sweet
    chocolate chips
1 cup creamy peanut butter
1 tablespoon butter or
    margarine
1½ cups crisp rice cereal

1. Preheat oven to 350°F. Grease bottom of 13×9-inch baking pan.

2. Prepare and bake brownies following package directions for cake-like recipe. Remove from oven. Sprinkle marshmallows on hot brownies. Return to oven. Bake for 3 minutes longer.

3. Place chocolate chips, peanut butter and butter in medium saucepan. Cook over low heat, stirring constantly, until chips are melted. Add rice cereal; mix well. Spread mixture over marshmallow layer. Refrigerate until chilled. Cut into bars.

Makes about 2 dozen bars

Tip: For a special presentation, cut cookies into diamond shapes.

Captivating Caterpillar Cupcakes

1 package DUNCAN HINES®
　Moist Deluxe® White
　Cake Mix

3 egg whites

1 ⅓ cups water

2 tablespoons vegetable oil

½ cup star decors, divided

1 container DUNCAN
　HINES® Vanilla Frosting

Green food coloring

6 chocolate sandwich
　cookies, finely crushed
　(see Tip)

½ cup candy-coated
　chocolate pieces

⅓ cup assorted jelly beans

Assorted nonpareil
　decors

1. Preheat oven to 350°F. Place 24 (2½-inch) paper liners in muffin cups.

2. Combine cake mix, egg whites, water and oil in large bowl. Beat at low speed with electric mixer until moistened. Beat at medium speed 2 minutes. Fold in ⅓ cup star decors. Fill paper liners about half full. Bake at 350°F 18 to 23 minutes or until toothpick inserted in center comes out clean. Cool in pans 5 minutes. Remove to cooling racks. Cool completely.

3. Tint vanilla frosting with green food coloring. Frost one cupcake. Sprinkle ½ teaspoon chocolate cookie crumbs on frosting. Arrange 4 candy-coated chocolate pieces to form caterpillar body. Place jelly bean at one end to form head. Attach remaining star and nonpareil decors with dots of frosting to form eyes. Repeat with remaining cupcakes. *Makes 24 cupcakes*

Tip: To finely crush chocolate sandwich cookies, place cookies in resealable plastic bag. Remove excess air from bag; seal. Press rolling pin on top of cookies to break into pieces. Continue pressing until evenly crushed.

Brownie Sundae Cake

1 (19- to 21-ounce) package fudge brownie mix, prepared according to package directions for cake-like brownies

1 cup "M&M's"® Semi-Sweet Chocolate Mini Baking Bits

½ cup chopped nuts, optional

1 quart vanilla ice cream, softened

¼ cup caramel or butterscotch ice cream topping

Line 2 (9-inch) round cake pans with aluminum foil, extending slightly over edges of pans. Lightly spray bottoms with vegetable cooking spray; set aside. Preheat oven as brownie mix package directs. Divide brownie batter evenly between pans; sprinkle ½ cup "M&M's"® Semi-Sweet Chocolate Mini Baking Bits and ¼ cup nuts, if desired, over each pan. Bake 23 to 25 minutes or until edges begin to pull away from sides of pan. Cool completely. Remove layers by lifting foil from pans.

To assemble cake, place one brownie layer, topping-side down, in 9-inch springform pan. Carefully spread ice cream over brownie layer; drizzle with ice cream topping. Place second brownie layer on top of ice cream layer, topping-side up; press down lightly. Wrap in plastic wrap and freeze until firm. Remove from freezer about 15 minutes before serving. Remove side of pan. Cut into wedges.

Makes 12 slices

Chocolate Peanut Butter Cups

1 package DUNCAN HINES® Moist Deluxe® Swiss Chocolate Cake Mix

1 container DUNCAN HINES® Creamy Home-Style Classic Vanilla Frosting

½ cup creamy peanut butter

15 miniature peanut butter cup candies, wrappers removed, cut in half vertically

1. Preheat oven to 350°F. Place 30 (2½-inch) paper liners in muffin cups.

2. Prepare, bake and cool cupcakes following package directions for basic recipe.

3. Combine vanilla frosting and peanut butter in medium bowl. Stir until smooth. Frost one cupcake. Decorate with peanut butter cup candy, cut-side down. Repeat with remaining cupcakes and candies.

Makes 30 servings

Brownie Sundae Cake

Merry-Go-Round Cake

1 package (6-serving size)
 JELL-O® Instant
 Pudding and Pie
 Filling, Vanilla Flavor
1 package (2-layer size)
 yellow cake mix
4 eggs
1 cup water
¼ cup vegetable oil
⅓ cup BAKER'S® Semi-
 Sweet Real Chocolate
 Chips, melted
⅔ cup cold milk
 Sprinkles (optional)
 Paper carousel roof
 (directions follow)
3 plastic straws
6 animal crackers

RESERVE ⅓ cup pudding mix. Combine cake mix, remaining pudding mix, eggs, water and oil in large bowl. Beat at low speed of electric mixer just to moisten, scraping sides of bowl often. Beat at medium speed 4 minutes. Pour ½ of the batter into greased and floured 10-inch fluted tube pan. Mix chocolate into remaining batter. Spoon over batter in pan; cut through with spatula in zigzag pattern to marbleize. Bake at 350°F for 50 minutes or until cake tester inserted in center comes out clean. Cool in pan 15 minutes. Remove from pan; finish cooling on rack.

BEAT reserved pudding mix and milk in small bowl until smooth. Spoon over top of cake to glaze. Garnish with sprinkles, if desired.

CUT 10- to 12-inch circle from colored paper; scallop edges, if desired. Make 1 slit to center. Overlap cut edges to form carousel roof; secure with tape. Cut straws in half; arrange on cake with animal crackers. Top with roof. *Makes 12 servings*

Prep Time: 30 minutes
Bake Time: 50 minutes

Merry-Go-Round Cake

Mini Turtle Cupcakes

1 package (21.5 ounces) brownie mix plus ingredients to prepare mix

½ cup chopped pecans

1 cup prepared or homemade dark chocolate frosting

½ cup chopped pecans, toasted

12 caramels, unwrapped

1 to 2 tablespoons whipping cream

1. Heat oven to 350°F. Line 54 mini (1½-inch) muffin cups with paper muffin cup liners.

2. Prepare brownie batter as directed on package. Stir in chopped pecans.

3. Spoon batter into prepared muffin cups filling ⅔ full. Bake 18 minutes or until toothpick inserted into centers comes out clean. Cool in pans on wire racks 5 minutes. Remove cupcakes to racks; cool completely. (At this point, cupcakes may be frozen up to 3 months. Thaw at room temperature before frosting.)

4. Spread frosting over cooled cupcakes; top with pecans.

5. Combine caramels and 1 tablespoon cream in small saucepan. Cook over low heat until caramels are melted and mixture is smooth, stirring constantly. Add additional 1 tablespoon cream if needed. Drizzle caramel decoratively over cupcakes. Store at room temperature up to 24 hours or cover and refrigerate for up to 3 days before serving.

Makes 54 mini cupcakes

Mini Turtle Cupcakes

Banana Split Cake

1 package DUNCAN HINES®
Moist Deluxe® Banana
Supreme Cake Mix

3 eggs

1⅓ cups water

½ cup all-purpose flour

⅓ cup vegetable oil

1 cup semi-sweet mini
chocolate chips

2 to 3 bananas

1 can (16 ounces)
chocolate syrup

1 container (8 ounces)
frozen whipped
topping, thawed

½ cup chopped walnuts

Colored sprinkles

Maraschino cherries with
stems, for garnish

1. Preheat oven to 350°F. Grease and flour 13×9×2-inch pan.

2. Combine cake mix, eggs, water, flour and oil in large bowl. Beat at low speed with electric mixer until moistened. Beat at medium speed 2 minutes. Stir in chocolate chips. Pour into pan. Bake at 350°F 32 to 35 minutes or until toothpick inserted in center comes out clean. Cool completely.

3. Slice bananas. Cut cake into squares; top with banana slices. Drizzle with chocolate syrup. Top with whipped topping, walnuts and sprinkles. Garnish with maraschino cherries.   *Makes 12 to 16 servings*

Tip: Dip bananas in diluted lemon juice to prevent darkening.

Fudgy Peanut Butter Cake

1 (18.25-ounce) box
chocolate fudge
cake mix

2 eggs

1½ cups plus ⅔ cup water,
divided

1 (16-ounce) package
chocolate fudge
frosting mix

1¼ cups SMUCKER'S® Chunky
Natural Peanut Butter
or LAURA SCUDDER'S®
Nutty Old-Fashioned
Peanut Butter

Grease and flour 10-inch tube pan. In large bowl, blend cake mix, eggs and 1½ cups water until moistened; mix as directed on cake package. Pour batter into pan.

In medium bowl, combine frosting mix, peanut butter and ⅔ cup water; blend until smooth. Spoon over batter in pan.

Bake in preheated 350°F oven 35 to 45 minutes or until top springs back when touched lightly in center. Cool upright in pan 1 hour; remove from pan. Cool completely.   *Makes 12 to 15 servings*

Banana Split Cake

Sensations

Pretty In Pink Peppermint Cupcakes

1 package (18.25 ounces) white cake mix

1⅓ cups water

3 large egg whites

2 tablespoons vegetable oil or melted butter

½ teaspoon peppermint extract

3 to 4 drops red liquid food coloring *or* ¼ teaspoon gel food coloring

1 container (16 ounces) prepared vanilla frosting

½ cup crushed peppermint candies (about 16 candies)

1. Preheat oven to 350°F. Line 30 regular-size (2½-inch) muffin pan cups with pink or white paper muffin cup liners.

2. Beat cake mix, water, egg whites, oil, peppermint extract and food coloring with electric mixer at low speed 30 seconds. Beat at medium speed 2 minutes.

3. Spoon batter into prepared cups filling ¾ full. Bake 20 to 22 minutes or until toothpick inserted into centers comes out clean. Cool in pans on wire racks 10 minutes. Remove cupcakes to racks; cool completely. (At this point, cupcakes may be frozen up to 3 months. Thaw at room temperature before frosting.)

4. Spread cooled cupcakes with frosting; top with crushed candies. Store at room temperature up to 24 hours or cover and refrigerate up to 3 days before serving. *Makes about 30 cupcakes*

Pretty In Pink Peppermint Cupcakes

White Chocolate Raspberry Cake

1 package (6 squares)
   BAKER'S® Premium
   White Baking
   Chocolate, chopped
½ cup (1 stick) butter *or*
   margarine
1 package (2-layer size)
   white cake mix
1 cup milk
3 eggs
1 teaspoon vanilla
   White Chocolate Cream
   Cheese Frosting (page
   136)
2 tablespoons seedless
   raspberry jam
1 cup raspberries

HEAT oven to 350°F. Grease and flour 2 (9-inch) round cake pans; set aside.

MICROWAVE chocolate and butter in medium microwavable bowl on HIGH 2 minutes or until butter is melted. Stir until chocolate is completely melted; cool slightly.

BEAT cake mix, milk, eggs, vanilla and chocolate mixture in large bowl with electric mixer on low speed just until moistened, scraping side of bowl often. Beat on medium speed 2 minutes or until well blended. Pour into prepared pans.

BAKE 25 to 28 minutes or until toothpick inserted in center comes out clean. Cool cakes in pans 10 minutes; remove from pans. Cool completely on wire rack.

PLACE 1 cake layer on serving plate. Spread with ⅔ cup of the frosting, then jam. Place second cake layer on top. Frost top and side with remaining frosting. Garnish with raspberries.   *Makes 12 to 16 servings*

Marbled White Chocolate Raspberry Cake: Prepare batter as directed. Remove 1 cup batter to small bowl. Stir in 2 tablespoons seedless raspberry jam and 2 drops red food coloring. Spoon remaining batter into prepared pans. Place spoonfuls of pink batter into each pan. Swirl with small knife to marbleize. Bake as directed.

Prep Time: 30 minutes
Bake Time: 28 minutes

continued on page 136

White Chocolate Raspberry Cake

White Chocolate Raspberry Cake, continued

White Chocolate Cream Cheese Frosting

> 1 package (8 ounces) PHILADELPHIA® Cream Cheese, softened
> 4 tablespoons (½ stick) butter or margarine, softened
> 1 package (6 ounces) BAKER'S® Premium White Baking Chocolate, melted, cooled slightly
> 1 teaspoon vanilla
> 2 cups powdered sugar

BEAT cream cheese and butter in large bowl with electric mixer on medium speed until well blended. Add melted chocolate and vanilla; beat until blended.

BEAT in sugar until light and fluffy   *Makes 3 cups*

Prep Time: 10 minutes

Strawberry Celebration Cake

> 1 package DUNCAN HINES® Moist Deluxe® Strawberry Supreme Cake Mix
> 1 cup strawberry preserves, heated
> 1 container DUNCAN HINES® Creamy Home-Style Cream Cheese Frosting
> Strawberry halves, for garnish
> Mint leaves, for garnish

1. Preheat oven to 350°F. Grease and flour 10-inch Bundt or tube pan.

2. Prepare, bake and cool cake following package directions for basic recipe.

3. Split cake horizontally into three even layers. Place bottom cake layer on serving plate. Spread with ½ cup warm preserves. Repeat layering. Top with remaining cake layer. Frost cake with Cream Cheese frosting. Garnish with strawberry halves and mint leaves. Refrigerate until ready to serve.

Makes 12 to 16 servings

Tip: For a delicious variation, substitute 1 cup seedless red raspberry jam for the strawberry preserves.

Boston Cream Cheesecake

1 package (9 ounces)
    yellow cake mix
    (1 layer size)
2 packages (8 ounces
    each) PHILADELPHIA®
    Cream Cheese,
    softened
½ cup granulated sugar
2 teaspoons vanilla,
    divided
2 eggs
⅓ cup BREAKSTONE'S® or
    KNUDSEN® Sour Cream
2 squares BAKER'S®
    Unsweetened Baking
    Chocolate
3 tablespoons butter or
    margarine
2 tablespoons boiling
    water
1 cup powdered sugar

GREASE bottom of 9-inch springform pan. Prepare cake mix as directed on package; pour batter evenly into prepared springform pan. Bake at 350°F for 20 minutes.

BEAT cream cheese, granulated sugar and 1 teaspoon of the vanilla with electric mixer on medium speed until well blended. Add eggs, 1 at a time, mixing on low speed after each addition just until blended. Blend in sour cream; pour over cake layer.

BAKE an additional 35 minutes or until center is almost set. Run knife or metal spatula around rim of pan to loosen cake; cool before removing rim of pan.

MELT chocolate and butter in medium saucepan over low heat, stirring until smooth. Remove from heat. Add water, powdered sugar and remaining 1 teaspoon vanilla; mix well. Spread over cooled cheesecake. Refrigerate 4 hours or overnight.   *Makes 12 servings*

Prep Time: 25 minutes
Bake Time: 55 minutes

Double Berry Layer Cake

1 package DUNCAN HINES®
Moist Deluxe®
Strawberry Supreme
Cake Mix

⅔ cup strawberry jam,
divided

2½ cups fresh blueberries,
rinsed, drained and
divided

1 container (8 ounces)
frozen whipped
topping, thawed and
divided

Fresh strawberry slices,
for garnish

1. Preheat oven to 350°F. Grease and flour two 9-inch round cake pans.

2. Prepare, bake and cool cake following package directions for basic recipe.

3. Place one cake layer on serving plate. Spread with ⅓ cup strawberry jam. Arrange 1 cup blueberries on jam. Spread half the whipped topping to within ½ inch of cake edge. Place second cake layer on top. Repeat with remaining ⅓ cup strawberry jam, 1 cup blueberries and remaining whipped topping. Garnish with strawberry slices and remaining ½ cup blueberries. Refrigerate until ready to serve. *Makes 12 servings*

Tip: For best results, cut cake with serrated knife; clean knife after each slice.

Magical Tip

When purchasing blueberries, look for berries that are firm, plump, roughly uniform in size and indigo blue in color. Store blueberries, tightly covered, in the refrigerator for up to 10 days. Pick through the blueberries carefully before using, removing any moldy or shriveled berries and also removing any stems.

Double Berry Layer Cake

Chocolate Cream Torte

1 package DUNCAN HINES®
    Moist Deluxe® Devil's
    Food Cake Mix

1 package (8 ounces)
    cream cheese, softened

½ cup sugar

1 teaspoon vanilla extract

1 cup finely chopped
    pecans

1 cup whipping cream,
    chilled

    Strawberry halves for
    garnish

    Mint leaves for garnish

1. Preheat oven to 350°F. Grease and flour two 8- or 9-inch round cake pans.

2. Prepare, bake and cool cake following package directions for basic recipe. Chill layers for ease in splitting.

3. Place cream cheese, sugar and vanilla extract in small bowl. Beat at low speed with electric mixer until smooth. Add pecans; stir until blended. Set aside. Beat whipping cream in small bowl until stiff peaks form. Fold whipped cream into cream cheese mixture.

4. To assemble, split each cake layer in half horizontally (see Tip). Place one cake layer on serving plate. Spread top with one fourth of filling. Repeat with remaining layers and filling. Garnish with strawberry halves and mint leaves, if desired. Refrigerate until ready to serve.

Makes 12 to 16 servings

Tip: To split layers evenly, measure cake with ruler. Divide into 2 equal layers. Mark with toothpicks. Cut through layers with serrated knife, using toothpicks as guide.

Chocolate Cream Torte

Cobweb Cups

1 package (19.8 ounces) brownie mix plus ingredients to prepare mix

½ cup mini chocolate chips

2 ounces cream cheese, softened

1 egg

2 tablespoons sugar

2 tablespoons all-purpose flour

¼ teaspoon vanilla

1. Preheat oven to 350°F. Line 18 regular-size (2½-inch) muffin cups with paper muffin cup liners. Prepare brownie mix according to package directions for cakelike brownies. Stir in chocolate chips. Spoon batter into prepared muffin pans, dividing evenly.

2. Combine cream cheese and egg in small bowl; beat until well combined. Add sugar, flour and vanilla; beat until well combined.

3. Place cream cheese mixture in resealable plastic food storage bag; seal bag. With scissors, snip off small corner from one side of bag. Pipe cream cheese mixture in concentric circle design on each cupcake; draw toothpick through cream cheese mixture, out from center, 6 to 8 times.

4. Bake 20 to 25 minutes or until toothpick inserted into centers comes out clean. Cool in pans on wire racks 15 minutes. Remove to racks; cool completely.

Makes 18 cupcakes

Magical Tip

To soften cream cheese quickly, remove from the wrapper and place in a medium microwave-safe bowl. Microwave on MEDIUM (50% power) 15 to 20 seconds or until slightly softened.

Cobweb Cups

Pumpkin Chiffon Cake

CAKE

- 1 package DUNCAN HINES® Moist Deluxe® Spice Cake Mix
- 3 eggs
- 1 cup water
- 1 tablespoon vegetable oil plus additional for greasing
- 1 ½ cups solid pack pumpkin, divided

FILLING

- 2 cups whipping cream, chilled
- ½ cup sugar
- 1 cup Sugared Pecans, chopped (recipe follows)
- Sugared Pecan halves, for garnish

1. Preheat oven to 350°F. Grease and flour two 8-inch round cake pans.

2. For cake, combine cake mix, eggs, water and oil in large bowl. Beat at low speed with electric mixer until moistened. Beat at medium speed for 2 minutes. Fold in 1 cup pumpkin. Pour batter into pans. Bake and cool cake following package directions.

3. For filling, place whipping cream and sugar in large bowl. Beat at high speed with electric mixer until stiff peaks form. Fold in remaining ½ cup pumpkin and chopped Sugared Pecans.

4. To assemble, level cake layers. Split each cake layer in half horizontally. Place 1 cake layer on serving plate. Spread with one-fourth the filling. Repeat layering 3 more times. Garnish with Sugared Pecan halves.

Makes 12 to 16 servings

Sugared Pecans

- 1 cup sugar
- 1 tablespoon ground cinnamon
- 1 teaspoon salt
- 1 egg white
- 1 tablespoon water
- 1 pound pecan halves

1. Preheat oven to 300°F. Combine sugar, cinnamon and salt in small bowl; set aside.

2. Place egg white and water in medium bowl. Beat with electric mixer at medium speed until frothy but not stiff. Pour pecans into egg white mixture; stir until coated. Add sugar mixture; stir until evenly coated. Spread on cookie sheet. Bake at 300°F for 45 minutes, stirring every 15 minutes. Cool completely.

Pumpkin Chiffon Cake

Cappuccino Cake

½ cup (3 ounces) semisweet chocolate chips

½ cup chopped hazelnuts, walnuts or pecans

1 (18.25-ounce) package yellow cake mix

¼ cup instant espresso coffee powder

2 teaspoons ground cinnamon

1¼ cups water

3 large eggs

⅓ cup FILIPPO BERIO® Pure or Extra Light Tasting Olive Oil

Powdered sugar

1 (15-ounce) container ricotta cheese

2 teaspoons granulated sugar

Additional ground cinnamon

Preheat oven to 325°F. Grease 10-inch (12-cup) Bundt pan or 10-inch tube pan with olive oil. Sprinkle lightly with flour.

In small bowl, combine chocolate chips and hazelnuts. Spoon evenly into bottom of prepared pan.

In large bowl, combine cake mix, coffee powder and 2 teaspoons cinnamon. Add water, eggs and olive oil. Beat with electric mixer at low speed until dry ingredients are moistened. Beat at medium speed 2 minutes. Pour batter over topping in pan.

Bake 60 minutes or until toothpick inserted in center comes out clean. Cool on wire rack 15 minutes. Remove from pan. Place cake, fluted side up, on serving plate. Cool completely. Sprinkle with powdered sugar.

In medium bowl, combine ricotta cheese and granulated sugar. Sprinkle with cinnamon. Serve alongside slices of cake. Serve cake with cappuccino, espresso or your favorite coffee, if desired.

Makes 12 to 16 servings

Cappuccino Cake

146

Holiday Thumbprint Cookies

1 package (8 ounces) sugar-free, low-fat yellow cake mix

3 tablespoons orange juice

2 teaspoons grated orange peel

½ teaspoon vanilla

4 teaspoons strawberry all-fruit spread

2 tablespoons pecans, chopped

Preheat oven to 350°F. Spray baking sheets with nonstick cooking spray.

Beat cake mix, orange juice, orange peel and vanilla in medium bowl with electric mixer at medium speed for 2 minutes until mixture looks crumbly. Increase speed to medium and beat 2 minutes or until smooth dough forms. *Dough will be very sticky.*

Coat hands with nonstick cooking spray. Roll dough into 1-inch balls. Place balls 2½ inches apart on prepared baking sheets. Press center of each ball with thumb. Fill each thumbprint with ¼ teaspoon fruit spread. Sprinkle with nuts.

Bake 8 to 9 minutes or until cookies are light golden brown and lose their shininess. *Do not overbake.* Remove to wire racks; cool completely.

Makes 20 cookies

Holiday Thumbprint Cookies

Orange Dream Cake

¾ cup MIRACLE WHIP®
   Salad Dressing

1 (two-layer) yellow cake
   mix

1 envelope DREAM WHIP®
   Whipped Topping Mix

¾ cup orange juice

3 eggs

2 teaspoons grated orange
   peel

1½ cups powdered sugar

2 tablespoons milk

1 tablespoon multicolored
   sprinkles

- **BEAT** salad dressing, cake mix, whipped topping mix, juice, eggs and peel at medium speed with electric mixer for 2 minutes. Pour into greased and floured 10-inch fluted tube pan.

- **BAKE** at 350°F for 35 to 40 minutes or until wooden toothpick inserted near center comes out clean. Let stand 10 minutes; remove from pan. Cool.

- **STIR** together powdered sugar and milk until smooth. Drizzle over cake. Decorate with sprinkles.

Makes 8 to 10 servings

Prep Time: 10 minutes
Bake Time: 40 minutes

Blueberry Angel Food Cake Rolls

1 package DUNCAN HINES®
   Angel Food Cake Mix

¼ cup confectioners' sugar
   plus additional for
   dusting

1 (21-ounce) can blueberry
   pie filling

   Mint leaves for garnish
   (optional)

Preheat oven to 350°F. Line two 15½×10½×1-inch jelly-roll pans with aluminum foil.

Prepare cake mix as directed on package. Divide and spread evenly into pans. Cut through batter with knife or spatula to remove large air bubbles. Bake 15 minutes or until set. Invert cakes at once onto clean, lint-free dishtowels dusted with sugar. Remove foil carefully. Roll up each cake with towel jelly-roll fashion, starting at short end. Cool completely.

Unroll cakes. Spread about 1 cup blueberry pie filling to within 1 inch of edges on each cake. Reroll and place seam-side down on serving plate. Dust with ¼ cup sugar. Garnish with mint leaves, if desired.

Makes 2 cakes (8 servings each)

Tip: For a variation in flavor, substitute cherry pie filling for the blueberry pie filling.

Easy Egg Nog Pound Cake

1 (18¼-ounce) package yellow cake mix

1 (4-serving size) package instant vanilla flavor pudding and pie filling mix

¾ cup BORDEN® Egg Nog

¾ cup vegetable oil

4 eggs

½ teaspoon ground nutmeg

Powdered sugar (optional)

1. Preheat oven to 350°F.

2. In large mixing bowl, combine cake mix, pudding mix, Borden Egg Nog and oil; beat at low speed until moistened. Add eggs and nutmeg; beat at medium-high speed 4 minutes.

3. Pour into greased and floured 10-inch fluted or tube pan.

4. Bake 40 to 45 minutes or until toothpick inserted near center comes out clean.

5. Cool 10 minutes; remove from pan. Cool completely. Sprinkle with powdered sugar, if desired.

Makes 1 (10-inch) cake

Prep Time: 10 minutes
Bake Time: 40 to 45 minutes

Magical Tip

Ingredients for baking cakes should be at room temperature before mixing (unless the recipe directs otherwise). To warm up refrigerated eggs quickly, place the eggs in a bowl of warm—not hot—water for 5 to 10 minutes.

Christmas Rainbow Cake

1 package (2-layer size)
   white cake mix

1 package (4-serving size)
   JELL-O® Brand Lime
   Flavor Gelatin

1 package (4-serving size)
   JELL-O® Brand
   Strawberry Flavor
   Gelatin

2 tubs (8 ounces each)
   COOL WHIP® Whipped
   Topping, thawed

HEAT oven to 350°F.

PREPARE cake mix as directed on package. Divide batter equally between 2 bowls. Add lime gelatin to one bowl and strawberry gelatin to the other bowl. Stir until well blended. Pour each color batter into separate greased and floured 9-inch round cake pans.

BAKE 25 to 30 minutes or until toothpick inserted in center comes out clean. Cool 10 minutes; remove from pans. Cool to room temperature on wire racks.

SLICE each cooled cake layer in half horizontally. Place 1 lime-flavored cake layer on serving plate; frost with whipped topping. Top with 1 strawberry-flavored cake layer; frost with whipped topping. Repeat layers. Frost top and side of cake with remaining whipped topping.

Makes 10 to 12 servings

Storage Know-How: Store cakes frosted with COOL WHIP® Whipped Topping in the refrigerator.

Great Substitute: Use any two flavors of JELL-O® Brand Gelatin to fit your favorite holiday.

Prep Time: 30 minutes
Bake Time: 30 minutes

Christmas Rainbow Cake

Star Christmas Tree Cookies

COOKIES

- ½ **cup vegetable shortening**
- ⅓ **cup butter or margarine, softened**
- 2 **egg yolks**
- 1 **teaspoon vanilla extract**
- 1 **package DUNCAN HINES® Moist Deluxe® Classic Yellow or Devil's Food Cake Mix**
- 1 **tablespoon water**

FROSTING

- 1 **container (16 ounces) DUNCAN HINES® Creamy Home-Style Classic Vanilla Frosting**
- **Green food coloring**
- **Red and green sugar crystals for garnish**
- **Assorted colored candies and decors for garnish**

Preheat oven to 375°F. For cookies, combine shortening, butter, egg yolks and vanilla extract. Blend in cake mix gradually. Add 1 teaspoon water at a time until dough is rolling consistency. Divide dough into 4 balls. Flatten one ball with hand; roll to ⅛-inch thickness on lightly floured surface. Cut with graduated star cookie cutters. Repeat using remaining dough. Bake large cookies together on *ungreased* baking sheet. Bake 6 to 8 minutes or until edges are light golden brown. Cool cookies 1 minute. Remove from baking sheet. Repeat with smaller cookies, testing for doneness at minimum baking time.

For frosting, tint Vanilla frosting with green food coloring. Frost cookies and stack, beginning with largest cookies on bottom and ending with smallest cookies on top. Rotate cookies when stacking to alternate corners. Decorate as desired with colored sugar crystals and assorted colored candies and decors.

Makes 2 to 3 dozen cookies

Magical Tip

When baking more than one sheet of cookies at a time, rotate the baking sheets from front to back and top to bottom halfway through the baking time—this will compensate for any hot spots in the oven and insure even browning.

Star Christmas Tree Cookies

Acknowledgments

The publisher would like to thank the companies and organizations listed below for the use of their recipes and photographs in this publication.

Cherry Marketing Institute

CHIPS AHOY!® Chocolate Chip Cookies

ConAgra Grocery Products Company

Dole Food Company, Inc.

Duncan Hines® and Moist Deluxe® are registered trademarks of Aurora Foods Inc.

Eagle® Brand

Filippo Berio® Olive Oil

Grandma's® is a registered trademark of Mott's, Inc.

Hershey Foods Corporation

Kraft Foods Holdings

©Mars, Incorporated 2002

McIlhenny Company (TABASCO® brand Pepper Sauce)

Mott's® is a registered trademark of Mott's, Inc.

Nestlé USA

OREO® Chocolate Sandwich Cookies

The Quaker® Oatmeal Kitchens

The J.M. Smucker Company

Sunkist Growers, Inc.

Index

Index

159

METRIC CONVERSION CHART

VOLUME MEASUREMENTS (dry)

1/8 teaspoon = 0.5 mL
1/4 teaspoon = 1 mL
1/2 teaspoon = 2 mL
3/4 teaspoon = 4 mL
1 teaspoon = 5 mL
1 tablespoon = 15 mL
2 tablespoons = 30 mL
1/4 cup = 60 mL
1/3 cup = 75 mL
1/2 cup = 125 mL
2/3 cup = 150 mL
3/4 cup = 175 mL
1 cup = 250 mL
2 cups = 1 pint = 500 mL
3 cups = 750 mL
4 cups = 1 quart = 1 L

VOLUME MEASUREMENTS (fluid)

1 fluid ounce (2 tablespoons) = 30 mL
4 fluid ounces (1/2 cup) = 125 mL
8 fluid ounces (1 cup) = 250 mL
12 fluid ounces (1 1/2 cups) = 375 mL
16 fluid ounces (2 cups) = 500 mL

WEIGHTS (mass)

1/2 ounce = 15 g
1 ounce = 30 g
3 ounces = 90 g
4 ounces = 120 g
8 ounces = 225 g
10 ounces = 285 g
12 ounces = 360 g
16 ounces = 1 pound = 450 g

DIMENSIONS

1/16 inch = 2 mm
1/8 inch = 3 mm
1/4 inch = 6 mm
1/2 inch = 1.5 cm
3/4 inch = 2 cm
1 inch = 2.5 cm

OVEN TEMPERATURES

250°F = 120°C
275°F = 140°C
300°F = 150°C
325°F = 160°C
350°F = 180°C
375°F = 190°C
400°F = 200°C
425°F = 220°C
450°F = 230°C

BAKING PAN SIZES

Utensil	Size in Inches/Quarts	Metric Volume	Size in Centimeters
Baking or Cake Pan (square or rectangular)	8×8×2	2 L	20×20×5
	9×9×2	2.5 L	23×23×5
	12×8×2	3 L	30×20×5
	13×9×2	3.5 L	33×23×5
Loaf Pan	8×4×3	1.5 L	20×10×7
	9×5×3	2 L	23×13×7
Round Layer Cake Pan	8×1½	1.2 L	20×4
	9×1½	1.5 L	23×4
Pie Plate	8×1¼	750 mL	20×3
	9×1¼	1 L	23×3
Baking Dish or Casserole	1 quart	1 L	—
	1½ quart	1.5 L	—
	2 quart	2 L	—